DEDICATION

To My Grandchildren - Jess, Oskar, Liberty, Scarlet, Zach and Alanis.

May you enjoy many adventures in your lives.

Flying with The Little Prince

The date is the twenty-ninth of December and the year, 1935. The scene is the Aéroport de Paris, Le Bourget. It is the start of the Paris to Saigon air race, sponsored by the Aéro-Club de France, with a prize of 1.2 million French Francs.

The provision was that the race be completed in less than 90 hours for the charted distance of 13,800 miles, which would undoubtedly increase due to winds blowing competitors off course and diversions for weather or mechanical problems. This journey would require an average speed, over the ground, in excess of 150 miles per hour.

Antoine de Saint Exupéry chose to use his red and white Caudron C630 Simoun aircraft, registration F-ANRY, which had a top speed of 193 mph and a range of just over 750 miles – which was important, as one needed to avoid loss of time by minimising the number of refuelling stops.

Incidentally, the registration for Antoine's plane was no French administrative allocation of letters. He chose it himself, using the first two letters from 'Antoine' and the last two letters from 'Exupéry'. With a full name of Antoine Marie Jean-Baptiste Roger comte de Saint

Exupéry, it was little wonder that, outside of aristocratic circles, his friends knew him simply as 'Saint-Ex'.

Antoine chose André Prévot as his navigator and flight engineer for the race, pictured below standing to the left of Saint-Ex, in front of their single-engined Simoun C630, ready for the off.

Once airborne from Le Bourget, they followed the valley of the Loire, then crossed the south coast of France near Marseille, heading for Sardinia. While flying out across the Mediterranean Sea, they noticed fuel leaking from the left wing tank and were forced to return to the airfield of Marignane Berre, just inland from Marseille. The leak was repaired and the aircraft refuelled, but valuable time was irretrievably lost before the red and white Simoun took off again, routing direct to Tunis.

After refuelling in Tunis, Saint Exupéry and Prévot flew the Simoun to the Libyan port of Benghazi for a moonless night landing, guided to the runway by the airfield's red beacons. After twenty minutes to refuel their single-engine aircraft, they took off for a night flight direct to Cairo, which took an inland route that followed the coastline of North Africa. The flight should have taken three and a half hours, but after three hours of flying they encountered low cloud and were forced to descend to an estimated altitude of 1,300 feet as they searched for the lights of the Nile Valley. They were out of range for radio contact with any airfields so were unable to reset the pressure settings on their altimeter, meaning there could easily have been an error of 300 feet or more in the altitude readings from their cockpit instruments.

After four hours, assuming that they must have missed their destination, Saint Exupéry turned back to fly a north east heading, hoping to reach the coastline of North Africa. Thinking they could see a lighthouse beacon, they flew towards it in worsening visibility, while at the same time being forced ever lower by the thickening cloud base.

The aircraft met the gently rising terrain of the Sahara, skidding along at one hundred and seventy miles per hour, causing heavy damage to the Simoun C630. Both men were unhurt but their water supplies were lost, save for a pint of coffee, half a bottle of wine, some grapes, and a single orange. Not the ideal preparation for being lost in the Libyan desert.

Initially, they decided to stay with their stricken aircraft and walk each day, in differing directions, searching for water and help. They found neither. After two days, and having decided there was little hope of being found by a search party, they abandoned the wreck of their aircraft and walked until exhausted and dehydrated, with the early morning dew their only source of water.

Eventually resigned to dying in the desert, they collapsed, with their throats set hard and tongues like dried leather. That night was very cold in the open desert, and they had thrown away their coats, which would have provided some warmth and comfort. The next morning they decided to continue walking, as best they could, occasionally drifting off into hallucinations, at one time thinking they saw footprints in the sand – but these were no mirage, they would eventually discover. They scanned the horizon for signs of life without success.

It was as if the guardian angels of aviators decided that Saint Exupéry had not yet completed his life's work. A Beduoin and his camel appeared from behind a sand dune. He wasn't looking in their direction, and though Exupéry and Prévot waved their arms and shouted, only whispers came from their dry throats. Finally, the Bedouin turned his head, agonisingly slowly, and they were found.

Water. Life-saving water was given to them by the Bedouin, in bowls. He made them lie on their stomachs, lapping the water like dogs to avoid drinking too quickly.

Saint Exupéry's story was published in 1939 as *Terre des Hommes*, translated into English with the title *Wind, Sand and Stars*.

Antoine de Saint Exupéry is a famed French aviator, an accomplished and daring pilot for the Free French Air Force who later, along with other legendary French pilots, pioneered Aéropostale routes through North and West Africa from Morocco to Senegal and, later still, throughout South America. Although less well known by the British as a courageous and daring pilot, he will be familiar to many as the author of one of the best-selling books ever published, the delightful *Little Prince*, superficially a children's story which speaks to all of us through its wisdom and philosophy. *The Little Prince* story, written some six years after the event, is set in the Sahara Desert after his aircraft crash.

Saint-Ex was an author, a poet, and a philosopher. Anyone who has read his books – *Flight to Arras, Southern Mail, Night Flight*, or *Wind, Sand and Stars* – will understand the reasons why he was honoured with several of France's highest literary awards. For me he is a brave and exceptional pilot as well as author, whose life

interweaves with four tales of my own flying adventures in Libya, Senegal, Argentina, and Madagascar in a way which will become clearer as my stories progress.

My first story in the form of a travel diary is called, "Desert Foxes over Libya", and was written in 2009, at a time when Colonel Gaddafi was still running the country. With my Belgian friend, Bernard de Maeterlinck, I spent six days flying in Libya, over the Sahara Desert, and fortunately we were spared the fate of Saint Exupéry's unscheduled landing in the Sahara. It did mean, though, that we never had the chance to make the acquaintance of the Little Prince.

Desert Foxes over Libya
November 2009

We didn't see a desert fox, which I would like to have done. Also called the fennec fox, it is not much larger than a domestic cat and has large batwing ears to pick up the slightest sound of an insect or small rodent that might become its dinner. The desert fox is a hardy nocturnal survivor, who lives in probably as harsh an environment as there is in the world – the Sahara Desert. He was an excellent role model for our flying trip across the Libyan desert.

Day One: Friday afternoon, 20 November

Despite clear instruction for military precision on timekeeping, our 1600 hour briefing in the Hotel Gray d'Albion in Cannes did not commence until 1630. Ex-military man, Sam Rutherford, did have the good grace to apologise for not informing us of the delayed start to the briefing!

The crews of ten UK aircraft were assembled to hear about our flying adventure from Cannes to Tripoli, then around the eastern Sahara Desert. Of course, for most of us, our adventure had begun already with flights from England down the Rhone Valley in November – no mean feat in itself.

Day Two: Saturday 21 November

Saturday morning, and we had a 430nm flight to Tunis ahead of us. My Belgian co-pilot, Bernard Maeterlinck, and I had decided to break the journey in Figari, Corsica, to refuel. Our buddy aircraft, a Cessna 182 G-IJAG, flown by Deryck Sutton and Robin Wicks, filed the same flight plan.

Unfortunately, their C182 was twenty knots faster than our Piper Archer G-BOPA, and we were soon cast off as buddies for the faster and racier models of aircraft ahead! We settled for keeping Sam and Bea company in their Maule MX7 as the 'tail-end Charlies' of the squadron. Mark you, it did cost Deryck and Robin a few beers – at least when we could get beers, which was an option soon to disappear when we arrived in Libya.

The other eight aircraft, mostly single engines but with a couple of twins, all filed direct to Tunis. Unfortunately, there was a breakdown in air traffic communications; the Italians did not receive the flight plans, and permission was not granted to cross Italian airspace, so everyone

diverted to Figari. Competition for a cup of coffee and a sandwich became intense at the tiny snack bar, followed by lots of phone calls to flight planning!

Our second leg, and everyone else's now, took us over the mountainous island of Sardinia and on a 114 nautical miles sea crossing to North Africa, Tunisia, culminating with a landing on runway 19 at Tunis. Pilots with single engine planes are always aware that an engine failure while over the sea would involve an unwelcome landing on water. We wear life jackets and would have to radio our mayday call to alert the rescue services, but we accepted the small increase in risk because we never told the engine that we'd left the land behind and were now over water. Ten years earlier, when making my first sea crossing of the 21 miles of English Channel, I was less sanguine and climbed to 5,500 feet, so that an engine failure at the mid-point would still allow me to glide to France!

That night, we stayed at The Consul Hotel in Rue de Palestine and ate in the Medina. We were met at the entrance to the Medina by a tall Tunisian dressed in traditional robes and carrying a lantern to light our way through the labyrinthine streets. Our restaurant was a large room of beautiful Moorish architecture, set out with tables for dinner and a musician playing a lute-shaped guitar and singing unfamiliar songs. The singer did, however, bravely attempt an unusual but recognisable version of 'Happy Birthday' for Deryck Sutton.

Day Three: Sunday 22 November

Our flight from Tunis was delayed. We had arrived early to clear airport formalities, refuel, and leave promptly with the fastest planes first, starting with Dave Tucker and Mark Goodey in N154DJ, followed by Bill and Wendy Burton in G-CRUZ. With the last four slower aircraft on the taxiway, we were recalled to the apron by air traffic, as the Tunisian police were missing an exit stamp in one unidentified passport. It was never found, but the huffing and puffing of the Tunisian officials delayed us a further hour before we were airborne and on our way to Libya.

Our flight out of Tunisia was excellent, with the air traffic controller at Djerba, lacking the benefit of radar, asking for our distance and radial to his VOR radio beacon every two minutes! We crossed the Libyan border and entered Tripoli airspace at 2,500 feet, to maintain visual flight under the lowering cloud base.

After landing at the main Tripoli International airport, we were directed to taxi our aircraft (it seemed for miles) far from the terminal, to park up in a graveyard for huge Russian Ilyushin 76M cargo planes. So ten giant aircraft, in various states of decay, were the night's guardians for our ten gnat-size planes.

We were bussed to the terminal and the seemingly never-ending checks for swine flu, passports, bag scanning, passports again, and more bag scanning, before walking across a jam-packed and chaotic car park to our transfer coach. Thank goodness for cases with wheels.

On our drive through the centre of bustling and traffic-congested Tripoli we were fascinated to find that Colonel Gaddafi's desert encampment was behind a walled and fortified estate in the centre of the city. He could easily nip out for a chicken and couscous takeaway and be back home again in fifteen minutes!

Our four star hotel was the Diplomatic, or 'Deplomatic' as it was styled in its marketing brochure. Four star in Libya is somewhat at variance with one's European expectations, and the lift required pushing button 9 for the eighth floor! The gold, mirrored panelling and subdued lighting in the lift did make one wonder if we had strayed into a lap-dancing establishment. The shower did not work and nor did the key to the room, which necessitated going back to the ground floor reception for reprogramming, twice – which was a lengthy procedure. So a quick wash and down to the bar for non-alcoholic Becks beer, the first of many during our stay in Libya.

We walked through the bustling city of Tripoli, where it seems that everyone on the streets is male. Where do they keep all their women? We arrived at the Roman stone arch of Marcus Aurelius, built in 163 AD, and walked through to a delightful open air terrace restaurant, overlooking the illuminated arch, to be seated beneath bougainvillea and pomegranate trees.

In Tripoli, one is never far from yet another dominating poster photograph of Muammar al-Gaddafi, frequently sunglassed, either wearing his heavily decorated and gold-braided colonel's uniform, or in more traditional Arab robes, watching over his flock.

Later, lying in our beds, we fell asleep to the night sounds of a wedding party, with drums and the weaving music of the snake charmer pipes, followed by celebratory fireworks. I presume that some of the fireworks did not fall harmlessly to the ground, as we were awakened at 2.30am by the sound of fire engines.

It would be a poor business decision to sell alarm clocks in Tripoli, for at 6.15am one is awoken by the distant sounds of the muezzin calling his faithful to prayer, shortly followed by the calls from another minaret, apparently just next door, using an amplified wail to wake us all up a good five minutes ahead of the crowing cockerel. My GPS said sunrise was 0644 that day, but not according to the Muslim clergy!

Day Four: Monday 23 November

Today we planned to fly south, alongside the Algerian border, over the Sahara Desert, to Ghadames. We began with a long-winded trail through the officialdom at the main airport at Tripoli before being bussed to our aircraft graveyard, where our planes were parked up. There were low clouds and light rain, so Sam gave his briefing from inside the shell of one of the derelict Ilyushins. We stood in the cavernous and dusty shell of this old transport aircraft, with ransacked cables hanging from the exposed metal framework of the fuselage. Sam stood with his back to the cockpit that had been trashed by souvenir hunters, with the rain falling on the windscreen and pinging the aircraft's metal skin, while we made notes for our next routing.

We took off and climbed above the overcast cumulus cloud to 7,000 feet for the first 80nm, after which we could descend under scattered clouds, floating along at 3,000 feet, and fly over the desert. The landscape was never dull, with changing rock and sand formations, occasional camel trains or herds of goats, dry river beds and dirt roads.

The last 30nm into Ghadames was clear skies and 19 degrees Centigrade. We were booked into the luxury Das Ghadames hotel, which was well-presented and of Arabic design, with comfortable bedrooms shared with local ants picnicking in the corners of the tiled floors.

Surprisingly, there were no taxis in the town, so it was a walk to the historic old city. For an entrance fee of five dinars we could roam through the very narrow streets and peek into the tiny houses now preserved as a historic site. In the centre of the old town was a small shop and cafe, with its silver pot of mint tea keeping warm on the glowing embers of the open fire.

We walked for a while with Martin and Annette Gosling, and it was charming to see Martin still keen to take lots of photos of his lovely wife in this romantic location. Clearly many years together has simply bonded them more closely.

The town was developing a tourist trade, and we met the owner of a furniture shop who took us to the edge of the town in his car, where flat circular loaves of bread were being baked in the sand covering of a wood fire smouldering within a shallow pit. We removed our shoes and sat on the carpeted floor of the large tent, whose walls were covered with colourful fabric hangings. Cushions were scattered on the floor, and we ate the warm, slightly gritty, herb-flavoured bread, washed down with the ever-present mint tea. Delicious.

Day Five: Tuesday 24 November

Taking off from Ghadames was an opportunity for Sam to video each plane. Orbiting above the runway and calling "Go", as he turned on to an overhead finals heading, we began our take off run on runway 27, with a ten knot tail wind. It all seemed to work well, but the videos have become 'lost', so we will never know, for sure, how good they were.

G-BOPA always took off behind the Grumman AA5, with Bernard and me listening to the lovely warm Dorset tones of Greg Stevens, and his amiable passenger Jerry Gee, over the radio. We always expected our sleek Piper Archer to overtake them, but they quickly became a small dot on our horizon, never to be seen again, until we landed to find them refuelled and parked up!

Our flight to Ghat took almost three hours for our Piper Archer, which we spent watching the compacted sand of the desert, covered with the tyre tracks of seismic geology survey teams searching for still more oil. The colours of the sand dunes varied from bright yellow in the sunlight to softer oranges in the shadows, then rocky hills and stony outcrops and the occasional oil rigs. It was surprising to find that the desert was 1,500 to 2,000 feet above sea level.

We were advised to land on the taxiway at Ghat as this was in a better condition than the main 17 Left runway surface. Another tail wind and lots of float for the landing. We were now in the very south of Libya, close to the border with Niger.

A fleet of four wheel drive vehicles took us to lunch, set out upon a huge carpet in the desert, miles from anywhere and surrounded by rocky hills. After lunch, we got back into our 4x4s for the journey to a tented desert camp for the night. We each had our own tents, with walls draped in billowing, white, flower-patterned silk, which gave the impression of sleeping on a cloud.

Osman had a beautiful carpeted and cushioned open tent where we could peruse his silver wares and drink his sweet mint tea, for which I seemed to be getting a taste. I bought some silver bangles for my granddaughters. As the sun went down, so did the temperature, and with no clouds to act as a duvet in the sky, it became very cold in the desert at night. Paul, Martin, and Bill had thoughtfully brought their wives with them to address this problem. For the rest of the lads, it was time to sleep in woolly jumpers.

Day Six: Wednesday 25 November

We set off for a morning drive into the rocky mountains of the Akakus. The winds have sculpted these rocks so that they are lined and segmented, as if built from huge rock bricks assembled by mythical Libyan giants. The sandstorms have weathered the rocks into fantastic shapes – the crocodile head, the two old ladies out shopping, and the huge thumb balanced precariously on a big smooth boulder. Peter Osborn, a passenger in Nigel Jackson's smart Cirrus SR22, strode the rocks, sporting his blue Tuareg headdress as he searched the skies for birds that he might identify in his accompanying reference book.

Large tracts of sandy desert valleys wove in and out of the rocks, allowing our Tuareg drivers, headdressed and sun-glassed up, to demonstrate their rally driving skills, while their radios blared out their favourite Arabic music.

We found rock paintings of animals dating back some 3,000 years. We completed our 40km drive across the sand and met up again with the tarmac road for the 80kms back to Ghat. Stops were made for photos and in a shanty town to buy silver from street traders, examine dangerous dagger-shaped letter openers, and bargain fiercely for bangles and trinkets. Strangely, a red fire engine drove sedately past, clearly not looking for a fire. Lunch was again a picnic on the carpeted desert.

We arrived at Ghat airfield by 3.30pm and prepped our aircraft for the 200nm afternoon flight north east to the military airfield of Ubari. Sunset was in three hours and we had not yet started our engines. We briefed on the route from the tail of Sam's plane and began taxiing in the order of fastest aircraft first. BOPA, being one of the slowest, took off last, and it was unlikely that we would land in daylight.

The desert landscape varied from flat rock plateau through sandy desert over cliff faces of 3,000 feet, interspersed with dune fields with edges sharpened and colours enriched by the sinking orange sun. It was truly a dramatic and memorable flight, as we feasted our eyes on the stark beauty of the desert shadows in the lowering and reddening sun.

We landed fifteen minutes after sunset, onto the brightly illuminated runway at Ubari. Transport took us on a thirty minute drive to a camp of rondavel huts with straw coolie hat roofs. The accommodation was sparsely furnished, with distant communal shower and toilet facilities that fell well short of even a description of 'basic', or indeed clean. It was now that we realised a torch and toilet roll would have been useful additions to our luggage – but we survived, if rather unwashed.

The next morning, Barry Ledeatte, flying in G-PREZ with Ed Riley, enjoyed a bare-footed run across the dunes, leaving his 'first man' footprints for all to see.

Day Seven: Thursday 26th

Seven Toyota Land Cruisers took us four-wheel driving across the desert dunes at speeds up to 70 mph. It was an exhilarating ride over the world's largest rollercoaster. Weaving and side-slipping, climbing steep sandy slopes and rocking over the knife edge crest before plunging down the far side, black ski runs. We drove to the three saltwater Ashwari lakes in the middle of the Sahara Desert. From where the water comes, no-one seems to know, but they are oases surrounded by date palms and scrub bushes with a rickety cafe and sellers of souvenir silver jewellery. I couldn't resist yet another turban, or Cheche, this time in Libyan flag green to go with my black or white headdress options. Ed Riley chose a fetching metallic brown turban which, unfortunately, leaked the dye onto his moist forehead, as we found out later!

Seven of our team, led by Nigel, Bill, and Wendy, decided on a swim in the lake, with its buoyant water that curiously became warmer the deeper it went. Afterwards, with stinging eyes and bodies drying to a white salt coating, the swimmers dashed to the nearby fresh water showers to salve their itching skin.

Olly Reston, and his father, who had joined us for part of the trip in their Citation jet, even skied down one of the sand slopes, which behaved much like an alpine snow piste.

Libyan cuisine is not world-renowned unless you really like couscous, over-ripe banana, and inedible meat washed down with non-alcoholic Becks beer. Our most memorable meal was the Libyan-style stale baguette filled with cold omelette and chips. I was not alone in failing to finish this meal.

That evening I walked into what little there was of the town of Ubari with Mike McGinty, who was taking time off from his job of commanding the British Army helicopter fleet. Lucky he was with me, as I took a wrong turning on the way back to the camp and required Mike's field craft to find our way home.

Day Eight: Friday 27 November

In a desert country one might expect water to be a precious and husbanded commodity, but strangely, no. Water is used wastefully; leaking pipes seem not to be repaired. Perhaps it is the presence of the immense underground freshwater lake in the south Sahara, which has been piped to the cities and towns, that gives the feeling of permanent supply. Electric lights remain on during the whole night and all through the day. Power is cheap and plentiful for Libyans.

Today, we fly north from Ubari to Sebha. Our start was delayed as we awaited the promised camel rides, but the price increased threefold, so they got no business from anyone that day! Instead, we had fun taking photos of the Flying Farmers in their airline shirts and captain's bars. Paul Stephens, Martin Gosling, and Bill Burton formed the uniformed backdrop for Wendy, who sportingly agreed to be the main photographic interest with her provocative and sexy model poses. No sign of camera-shy Roz, however, who was hiding her large blue eyes from us again!

We met the German family of Johanna and Marcel Noller, with their two young daughters, Julia and Ronja, who were driving their vintage red fire engine, GRISU, from Munich to Cape Town. The vehicle was the wedding present from the bride's father, and the couple had spent five years planning this epic journey. It was this fire engine that we had seen earlier on our way back to Ghat from the Akakus mountains.

After take-off, we flew over the camp and waved to the fire engine family before overflying the Ashwari lakes for airborne photography. Landing on runway 13 at Sebha for refuelling, we were invited into the control tower,

where we found our air traffic controller had previously worked in Air Traffic Control at Bournemouth airfield. Small world. The Sebha control tower was dominated by a large photo of the 'Colonel' sitting, no doubt in the first class compartment of an airliner, flanked by the heavily moustached flight crew.

The 362nm flight back north to Tripoli was mostly flown at 8,500 feet, where the air was smoother. Sam and his team filmed our take off and initial flight. The three and a half hour flight saw many changes in the landscape. The rolling sand dunes, favoured by the *Lawrence of Arabia* film-makers, actually only make up about a third of the desert.

We landed, on runway 29, at the military airfield of Mitaga, in Tripoli, greatly simplifying the normal bureaucratic paperwork and checks of the large civil airfields. Back at the 'Deplomatic' Hotel, which we now realised was very luxurious, we enjoyed our first proper showers for three days!

Day Nine: Saturday 28 November

The departure procedures of the military at Tripoli Mitiga were simpler than the inbound experience at Tripoli International. We had filed nine aircraft as Fox Formation, BOPA being Fox 8, and we took off in echelon, one after the other, with no radio calls.

Sam's taildragger Maule aircraft, N410TX with 'Never Say Never' painted on its fuselage, did some air to air filming of CHIX, GOSL and BOPA over Libya.

We searched in vain for Roman ruins along the coast, but when over Tunisia we did find the town of El Gem, which boasts the second largest Roman amphitheatre, after Rome. It is huge and dominates the town.

We landed on runway 29 in Tunis Carthage airport, noticing the more developed economy of Tunisia compared with Libya. We took a taxi to the Medina but found it closed for the festival of Aed, which explained the street barbecues of sheep's heads! We took another taxi to the city centre for coffee at the Cafe de Paris, on the tree-lined boulevard, watching the trams run through the streets. Finally we arrived back to the Consul Hotel which, luckily, we could find ourselves, as our taxi driver had no idea at all! Farewell speeches accompanied the dinner for the Fox Formation, who had started as strangers and now were good friends.

Day Ten: Sunday 29 November

We filed for Cannes with Ajaccio as alternate. A sausage-shaped cold front lay over the west and south of France, so we were not sure that we could make it all the way to Cannes that day. Dave Tucker and Mark Goodey took Dan Tye in their Crusader and filed instrument flight rules direct to France, taking off ahead of the visual flight rules pack.

Weather at Ajaccio was fine, although Nigel chose to land his Cirrus for an overnight stay. The rest of the birds continued towards Cannes, with the exception

of Dave and Mark, who flew direct to Lyon at 10,000 feet. We maintained 6,500 feet until halfway across the Mediterranean, from Corsica to the French coast, when we had to descend to 4,000 feet to get under the thick bank of cloud at the head of the cold front.

We continued to drift down slowly to maintain visibility and were at 2,500 feet when we were handed over to Nice Approach. The controller was excellent and understood our problems with the weather front, vectoring us direct to Sierra Alpha point for runway 35 at Cannes. Our plan was thwarted by an instrument flight arriving, necessitating that we divert to hold over the sea at Sierra Whisky point. Bernard was not happy at being bumped by an instrument flight rules queue jumper! But, as the very heavy rain over Cannes was moving only slowly east, we were in a clear patch of weather at Sierra Whisky. I was happy orbiting in the sunshine.

Our clearance for number one on finals for Cannes Mandelieu came a bit too early, as the storm had not yet departed Cannes. Bernard battled the gusts and heavy rain of the tail end of the storm until, at 800 feet, we could see the flashing strobes and red threshold runway lights – but we were too close, too high, and too fast for a textbook approach. The option of a go-around into the storm and mountains behind Cannes was not an appealing alternative, so we cleared the threshold, being 300 feet too high and 20 knots too fast. Bernard's problem was trying to reduce power to lose height and speed whilst simultaneously applying additional power to counteract the wind shear and maintain control of the aircraft.

Cannes, luckily, has a long runway of 1610 metres, and we used all of it, touching down halfway, not using the brakes on the wet runway, but stopping just yards from the end. We exited and joined the taxiway to the parking with a measure of relief and thanks to expert piloting by Bernard. Never Say Never was twenty minutes behind us and wondered what all the fuss was about, as Sam landed in bright sunshine!

The hot showers at the hotel felt wonderful after eight days of widely varying bathroom facilities.

Drinks at the Irish pub at 6.30pm, and we said our goodbyes to the good friends we had made on this trip, before enjoying an Italian pizza and bottle of Valpolicella with Deryck and Robin in a delightful family-run trattoria.

The Desert Foxes had completed a real Saharan adventure, excellently planned and managed, and enjoying the camaraderie of our fellow piolts. All we had to do now was fly back through France to Denham, Bournemouth, or Kortrijk, at the end of November. No problem!

Thank you, Sam and Bea, and your support teams. It was magical and a truly memorable experience.

For my second story we move on three years, to 2012, and begin following the aerial trails of Antoine de Saint Exupéry and the other French Aéropostale pilots.

Pierre-George Latécoère, born in 1883, was the son of a sawmill owner, whose business was located just to the south west of Toulouse. Pierre-George, following the attainment of his degree in manufacturing and technology, transformed his father's business to one specialising in the production of railway locomotives. The First World War provided the opportunity of large government contracts for the railway engines, as well as one order for 600 Salmson reconnaissance biplanes for the French Army. A new aircraft factory was built in Toulouse, within the suburb of Montaudran, establishing an aviation industry that continues today with Airbus Industrie.

With the end of the First World War, the orders for aircraft and locomotives dried up, and the Latécoère factory and skilled workforce needed a new source of revenue. Pierre-George saw the potential market for delivery of mail by air, significantly reducing the time taken for letters to reach the French colonies in North and West Africa, by both land and sea. Commencing with redundant Breguet 14 biplanes from the war, and later designing and developing a range of new Latécoère aircraft, the French Aéropostale service was started in 1918, a business that eventually would become one of the founder companies of Air France.

It was in October 2012 that I joined my friend Alistair Moon, flying with a French group of pilots, "Raid Latécoère", in West Africa. This Latécoère Rally is a French aeroclub and charity formed in 2007 to keep alive the memory of the Latécoère Airmail Service, its pilots amongst whom was Saint Exupéry and the aviation heritage of France.

As an aside, the name of Antoine de Saint Exupéry is written variously with and without a hyphen between 'Saint' and 'Exupéry'. I have chosen the original French spelling. The hyphen was introduced by Antoine during his visit to the United States in 1941. Becoming tired of being introduced as Mr. Exupéry, he changed the spelling to 'Saint-Exupéry'.

This second story is called "Third Time Unlucky" and recounts our flights retracing the routes flown by Antoine de Saint Exupéry, amongst others, in delivering airmail to the French colonies of Morocco, Mauritania, Senegal, and Côte d'Ivoire.

Third Time Unlucky
Flying in West Africa

France to Senegal and Back
October 2012

The Journey

The aircraft we were flying to Senegal was home built, from a kit, which might make one think of boyhood efforts to build cars, cranes, and planes out of the Meccano set delivered by Father Christmas. But that would be a grossly distorted picture to have in mind. The aircraft was designed by professional aviation engineers from the French Dyn'Aéro company. We were flying the four seat version of the lightweight carbon composite aircraft, the MCR4S with the registration of F-PLAN, and it flew remarkably well on the 100hp Rotax engine.

But all engineering equipment involves maintenance and adjustment and that became clear on our first check flight from Gaillac airfield in southern France. Everything appeared to work; she flew well and landed smoothly, but then the control column started juddering wildly after touch-down, as the nose wheel vibrated almost out of control. Back in the hangar, we discovered that two tensioning springs, designed to stop nose wheel vibration, had become detached. Reattached and tensioned, the problem was solved. We thought nothing more about it.

It was about two weeks later, on our way back from Senegal, that the next incident occurred. We had flown across Mauritania, stopping overnight in Dakhla. On the following day, the first leg took us to the north of Western

Sahara where, at La Ayoune, we refuelled to complete the second leg of the long day's flying to Agadir. Preparing for take-off, we started the engine and noticed a red warning light on the instrument panel. This was telling us that the battery was not charging and was a cause for concern. We shut the engine down and began checking for the fault. We quickly found that a couple of key electrical wires had become detached, and reconnecting them solved the problem so we could continue on our route home.

Thinking about it later makes me wonder if F-PLAN was trying to tell us something, but we failed to take notice of her second warning message.

But let me start at the beginning.

I first met Alistair on a flying safari to Cape Town and back home, in 2011. We were flying in separate aircraft but hit it off during the two month journey and, later, when back in Europe, he invited me to join the Raid Latécoère rally to West Africa.

Raid Latécoère is a group of French pilots that seeks to retrace the route of the French Aéropostale pioneers of the 1920s and 30s. The Aéropostale company was founded by Pierre-George Latécoère in 1918 and many famous French pilots flew for the business, including Jean Mermoz, Henri Guillaumet, and Antoine de Saint Exupéry. The French colonies in North and West Africa were accessible by flying south through Spain, across the straits of Gibraltar, to Morocco. It was this route, following the coastline south to Senegal, that Raid Latécoère was retracing. In addition, the Raid has a humanitarian role in raising money in support of schools in the former French colonies.

Alistair lives in the south of France at Gaillac, just to the north east of Toulouse, and it was his MCR4S aircraft that we were flying to Senegal and back.

I decided to drive to Alistair's chateau (he used to have his own vineyard) and leave my car at his place as we set forth on our three week adventure in the company of eleven other French aircraft.

Our starting point was Lézignan-Corbières, one of the Latécoère staging posts, and a thirty-five minute flight from Gaillac over the Black Mountains. It was here that we met the leader of the Raid, commercial pilot Hervé Berardi, who issued us with our hats, T-shirts, and fleece jackets, all bearing the logo of Raid Latécoère. The following day was set aside for briefings and getting to know our companions for the journey.

Saturday, the 6th October, was the day for departure and a flight to Almeria in the south of Spain. The aircraft were fuelled, prepared, and, being French, were each supplied with cheese, paté, and the baguette essentials for the journey. Our departure from Lézignan was scheduled for 9am, but low cloud and sea fog delayed us. Then, around 11am, a hole opened up above the airfield, with blue sky peeking through. We circled above the airfield, climbing around the puffy clouds until we got on top and were on our way.

Flying at 6,500 feet over the Low Pyrenees, then direct over the mountainous Spanish terrain, we arrived, four and a half hours later, in Almeria, where the Rambla is lined with palm trees. That evening, we ate tapas al fresco in a square amongst the Spanish families and their children, who were being amused by a man, dressed as a clown, making animals and swords from long thin sausage balloons. We had two large glasses of very acceptable red wine and four good-sized plates of hot tapas for only ten euros – and that was the tourist rate!

Our early breakfast and plans for a nine o'clock departure were thwarted by airport procedures and weather delays. Finally, Hervé was able to get his plane airborne and check the flying conditions, and he soon reported back by radio that it was clear for our take off, for flight to Fes. We climbed onboard, started engines, conducted all our pre-flight checks, and requested permission to taxi to the runway threshold. "Standby," replied the tower controller, and we stood by, sitting in our perspex canopy cockpit, getting hotter and hotter, waiting for air traffic clearance to depart.

We finally got away just after midday and flew along the Spanish coast until west of Malaga, then south across the Mediterranean overhead Gibraltar. The Rock stood out clearly above the low layer of cloud along the coast. We crossed the Moroccan border at Tetouan, then over the Atlas Mountains into the dry dusty plain for our landing at Fes. Morocco was as hot as our cockpit when on the apron at Almeria, as we put our clocks back two hours to North Africa time.

That evening, we visited the bustling market among the labyrinthine lanes of the Medina, where we were shown around a tile and pottery manufacturer, a leatherworks with the hides laid out in the sun, and saw coppersmiths beating large pans into shape whilst sitting cross-legged on the stone floor of their one small workshop.

Monday morning, and we prepared for our flight over the Atlas Mountains on our two and a half hour flight to Ouarzazate. We took off from Fes, and at 500 feet above the airfield, turned south west in a long climb to 7,500 feet, in the hot air of a cloudless sky. Curiously, as we climbed, the ground rose gently beneath us, so that we hardly ever flew much more than 500 feet above the ground to the top of the mountain range. It was a very bumpy flight, with thermals, mountain winds, and the occasional wiggle to avoid a rocky peak on our way to

Ouarzazate airfield, which lies in a dry and dusty plain at 3,800 feet above sea level.

The traditional post-flight beer tasted extra good that day. In the evening, we ate at the excellent Jardin d'Aromes restaurant. For starters, we were served with fifteen dishes of tapenades and other vegetarian savoury dips, which we ate with bread accompanied by rosé wine. The main course, placed in the centre of the table, arrived in a large silver dish covered with an ornate domed lid, which, when removed, revealed beef chunks in a dark sauce, garnished with apricots, prunes, boiled egg segments, and almonds. The sweet and appetising aroma made it irresistible. Lemon sorbet and melon with fresh mint leaves completed our meal. We headed for bed knowing we had to set our alarms for 5.30am next morning.

We need not have bothered setting our alarm, for the local muezzin began his wailing all too early. I wonder if this could be termed 'calling at an ungodly hour'!

It was the ninth of October, and we continued our journey through Morocco, with a flight to the west coast next morning that took nearly four hours until our landing at Tarfaya. This sand runway was the same one used by the Aéropostale pilots of the 1920s and 1930s

and is still operational. We were greeted with a glass of warm mint tea served to us inside a brightly coloured tent on the sand.

Tarfaya, known then as Cap Juby, was a refuelling stopover base for the Aéropostale service where Saint Exupéry was the station manager in 1927. It was during his time here that he wrote his first novel, "Southern Mail", when not being distracted by negotiations with the Moorish tribes demanding a ransom for the release of imprisoned pilots, unlucky enough to have made a forced landing in the desert.

The town is small, sad, and dusty, with piles of uncollected rubbish and pot-holed roads. All buildings seem either to be half-built, with little signs of further work in progress, or completed properties in various states of decay. Our hotel was basic – very basic. We drank coffee, awaiting soap, sheets for the bed, and towels.

Amazingly, if we had flown west, across the Atlantic Ocean, from this fishing port we would have been in the Canary Islands within one hundred miles.

We had two long flying days ahead of us, crossing Western Sahara and Mauritania to get to Senegal. Western Sahara was a Spanish colony, known as Spanish Sahara until the death of General Franco in 1975. The Moroccan army, together with 30,000 unarmed Moroccans, converged on Tarfaya, in what was known as the Green March, and pressured Spain into ceding the territory to Morocco. A year later, a guerrilla war erupted between Western Sahara separatists and Morocco that only halted in 1991, when the United Nations took control to maintain the peace and supervise a referendum to determine the will of the people for independence or to remain with Morocco. The UN is still in Western Sahara, it is still peaceful and still waiting, twenty-one years later, for the referendum.

Our first leg out from Tarfaya was a short hop to La Ayoune, where we refuelled our aircraft from steel drums. Back in the air, we found low cloud along the coastline so flew above it at 1200 feet, wondering if the cloud would clear and allow us to land at Dakhla. As we approached the finger of land upon which Dakhla sits, at the tip, the cloud kindly dispersed and we landed into a gusty wind on the northerly runway, hot and tired. After our fish dinner, we had an early night in preparation for the following day.

Thursday proved to be a very long and, flying into the relentless sun, extremely hot day in the perspex-domed cockpit, where there was no shade. From Dakhla to our refuel stop in Nouakchott took over three and a half hours. We were welcomed to Mauritania by staff of the Government Tourist Board encouraging us to come to Mauritania for a holiday. As there is little to see or do in Mauritania, unless you just can't get enough of desert sands, the task before the marketing team was somewhat challenging. Finally, they must have decided that the key selling point for Mauritania was that there was nothing there and came up with the memorable strap line of 'The Space on Earth'. A stroke of genius!

Our instructions for Mauritania were at odds with the holiday destination concept. We were told that should anything happen whilst at Nouakchott airfield, "Do not leave the airfield under any circumstances. Sleep in the terminal building if necessary". As if to support the view that Mauritania was not an altogether safe place, the president was shot in the arm by his own bodyguard while we were there – accidentally shot, it was said! No word as to the whereabouts or fate of the accident-prone bodyguard has been released since then.

After refuelling our aircraft, again from steel drums using a hand pump, it was four o'clock in the afternoon by the time we got airborne again for the two and a quarter hour flight to Dakar in Senegal. Our concern was to land in Senegal before sunset, as darkness comes quickly in the tropics, with very little twilight. We had the good fortune of a tail wind, but even as it pushed us along through the heat, we drank nearly two litres of water each. For the last two hours we resorted to taping our paper navigation charts to the perspex canopy of the cockpit, as keeping the sun out was preferable to seeing where we were going! I was exhausted by the time I arrived and welcomed the rest day on Friday.

Looking back, I am certain that I had become dehydrated in the challenging conditions. Alistair clearly has a more robust constitution for, the next day, he was off on a trip to the Isle de Goreé in the midday sun, while I spent the day sleeping, drinking water, and recovering in a darkened room.

Wow! What a day we had on Saturday. We flew to Ziguinchor, in the south of Senegal, passing over the marsh flats with small mangrove-like trees growing in the shallow waters, interspersed with cultivated rice fields. We loaded into three minibuses and set off in convoy with three Gendarmerie vehicles bristling with gendarmes in full battle dress and toting automatic weapons. We had an hour's drive through bandit country, passing roadside stalls selling fresh fish, fruit, and vegetables, to visit a village school at Soutou.

We were greeted enthusiastically by the pupils and staff of this small rural school, who had been waiting for our arrival. We were entertained with songs and dances for an hour before the official welcoming ceremony. Many speeches were delivered from the village chief through to the director of the school, after which our gifts to the school were presented. Following an informal game of football on a dirt pitch, we were fed lunch of rice, onion yassa, and grilled meat, all cooked outdoors over open fires and eaten under the shade of the playground trees. The day was emotional, rewarding, and it was humbling to see the eagerness and enthusiasm of the pupils and the dedication of the teachers and volunteer helpers. A day that will not be forgotten.

The flight, on Sunday, to the capital of The Gambia, Banjul, was only thirty minutes, as we now headed north and began our long journey home. We were joined for this flight by a goodwill escort aircraft from the Senegal Air Force. Their plane was an Epsilon single-engine propeller trainer with two seats in tandem.

Our welcome at Banjul Airport began with a television interview from the cockpit of our aircraft, before being besieged by officials requiring paperwork duties to be performed. The French Chargé d'Affaires was there to greet the Raid. Awaiting us, in front of the terminal building, were children in school uniform (remember it is a Sunday) who were waving flags and singing songs of greeting. Alongside was a troupe of dancers and drummers dressed in grass skirts, complete with witch doctor and the mythological Kumpa – a man dressed as a dancing haystack. The performance lasted twenty minutes and included a contortionist and fire-eater that would not disgrace the Cirque du Soleil, accompanied by the pulsating and insistent rhythms of the drums.

The streets of Banjul have wooden beds for sale along the sandy roadsides, lots of them, locally made in the open wooden sheds that are set back from the road; then more beds for sale on the next street. I saw no other furniture. No tables, no chairs, no cupboards, only beds. Is it possible that all Gambians have breakfast in bed?

We attended an official reception that evening, where we heard speeches from the French chargé d'affaires and the American ambassador. I got to meet the headmistress of Saint Therese's School, Zono Jemmeh, who is responsible for 2,300 students and 84 staff. She is a tall and intelligent lady, emanating warmth and caring, and was dressed in a long, elegant Gambian dress with matching cloth for her turban. She told me that she has five daughters and two younger sons, in addition to her career as a headmistress. Quite a lady.

We had a morning visit to the large secondary school of St Therese in Banjul, where we were guests of honour at the morning assembly, held on the concrete platform set in the middle of the dirt playground of the school. We heard speeches from the staff, various pupils, Hervé, and a talk from one of the pilots on the Raid, instructor and commercially qualified Carole Descazeaux, who spoke as a role model to the girls in the school, encouraging them to aim high and realise their dreams for the future.

One of the schoolboys approached me after assembly asking how he could become a pilot. A few days later I received this lovely email which I reproduce exactly as it was written:

"hello my dear friend MR DEREK, is MATARR NJIE from the GAMBIA student of SAINT THERESES SCHOOL whom you meet for comming to our country GAMBIA, am very much happy to write you this letter, hope you r hope you will read it with happiness".

It did make me happy and I replied with thanks. That afternoon we flew to St Louis, in northern Senegal.

And now it was Tuesday morning and yet another astonishing day in store for us. We took the coach to the ramshackle town on the main island of St Louis. We got out of the bus at the entrance to a small side street between the buildings, some in reasonable repair but some not. Imagine this sand street with the left hand side thronged with schoolgirls, clad in pink tabards, with ages ranging from three years upwards. Then the right hand side of the street was filled with boys dressed in dark blue tabards and both lines stretched the one hundred yards or more to the school entrance. There must have been close to a thousand children, chanting and cheering in time to the rhythm of the drummers.

As special guests, we walked between the schoolchildren's guard of honour, shaking as many hands as possible, laughing, overwhelmed, and a little tearful whilst wishing 'bonjour' and 'ça va' to as many as possible too. As we reached the school entrance, with all the children in a crowd behind us, our hands were grabbed and we floated into the school on this sea of happy pink and blue children. Not many days like that in your life.

There were many horse-drawn carriages, rustic and worn, in St Louis, which were ideal for short journeys or tourist rides around the dusty and ram-shackle fishing port. My attention was caught by an advertising board on the back of one of the carriages, which touted the benefits of a local hotel that offered WiFi, Aircon, and Marriage in that order. Maybe this offered a clue to the priorities of modern living?

That evening, we had dinner under the stars in the hot and humid evening air of St Louis, with everyone perfumed up with generous helpings of mosquito spray. We had a band to entertain us after the meal, and the younger members of the Raid soon were dancing to the foot-tapping rhythms from the Senegalese musicians. My better judgement failed me when I decided to join in the dancing. Much credit went to Christophe's pretty young Parisian girlfriend, Catherine, who not only agreed to accompany me but remained remarkably composed as I attempted to recreate moves from my own yesteryears with somewhat less than one hundred percent success. Well done, Catherine, for being so gracious whilst dancing with your 'Grandfather', and thank you, Hervé, for the mock administration of CPR chest compression, in case my heart had decided it had pumped enough blood for one evening!

The French pilots were excellent company and very tolerant of my agricultural pronunciation, which mangled their language. My face reminded them of a character from an old black and white film portraying an RAF pilot during the Second World War, shot down over France and seeking to make contact with the French resistance movement. I guess it was my moustache and English accent that allowed them to see a passing resemblance to Terry Thomas. True, I do have a small gap between my front teeth, but I would have selected Tom Selleck or Harrison Ford as my personal choice of look-a-like!

The RAF pilot in the film, complete with handlebar moustache, was told that the recognition code from the Resistance operatives would be the tune of 'Tea for Two'. So it was that I would be greeted by any gathering of the Raid Latecoere pilots with them whistling 'Tea for Two', followed by huge welcoming smiles. One evening I was joined at the dinner table by Alex, Greg, and Thibaut, all sporting impressive moustaches they had carved out of their ten days of unshaven facial hair – and, of course, a rendition of 'Tea for Two'. Great fun.

The following morning we left the colourful, crescent-shaped boats of St Louis behind as we continued our northerly journey home. First stop was at Nouakchott in Mauritania to refuel, which fortunately went without incident, and we set off on the second leg of our journey that day. We took thirty minutes to climb to the cooler air at 8,500 feet while we flew over seemingly endless miles of featureless desert. Occasionally, we would see a small fishing community, twenty or thirty shacks, without a tree or a square inch of shade to provide relief from the remorseless sun. The fishing boats were small open vessels with no protection from the burning Saharan sun.

Three and a half hours later we were back in Moroccan-administered Western Sahara at Dakhla, in the Sahara Regent hotel, with white United Nations 4x4s parked up outside. Peace was even monitored at our hotel, it would seem.

Thursday 18 October, two happy pilots made an early start from Dakhla and enjoyed a smooth flight for two and a half hours to La Ayoune for refuelling. Next stop, Agadir. And that was when our adventure took a surprising turn – not for the better. With our engine now fully operational, after resolving the problem with the non-charging battery, and now well behind schedule with most of our friends already airborne, we began the long taxi to the take-off threshold, which was over a kilometre away from the apron parking. It was when we were two thirds along the taxiway that we heard a 'BANG' outside the aircraft and she pulled to the right with a flat tyre. It was the starboard main landing wheel, and there was something about the sound of the 'BANG' that made us wonder if this was more than just a puncture. And so it transpired as we got out to inspect the damage. It was more than a flat tyre – the whole wheel had collapsed! Now we were well and truly stuck and a long way from help and home. Third time was really unlucky for us.

We had three other aircraft behind us, which were blocked. Somehow, with help from the other pilots, we lifted the crippled plane, its wings heavy with fuel, to the side of the taxiway to allow the other aircraft to taxi past our stricken craft. What to do? Franck Lagarrigue, the Raid engineer, and pilot Océan de Rancourt stayed to help us. A team of soldiers from the army, who shared this airfield with the commercial traffic, arrived, and with the aid of a pallet trolley and using some old tyres as a makeshift leg, we made the temporary wheel to get our aircraft back to the apron.

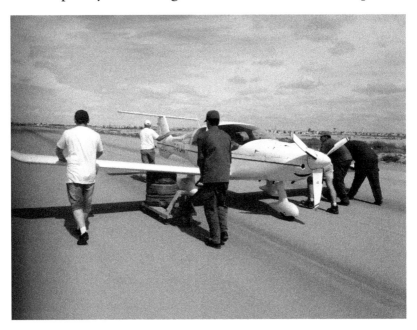

Not much more that Franck and Océan could do, so they took off in their plane, Delta Echo, to catch up with the rest of the Raid aircraft.

The end of this story has not yet been reached, but we do know the tyre burst when the wheel structure collapsed, and a new wheel assembly has been ordered from Dyn'Aéro for courier delivery to MDS Aviation engineering at Casablanca airfield. For now, we wait in La Ayoune in a hotel with air con and WiFi, but no beer for our traditional post-flight drink!

Enquiries revealed that there was one hotel in the town that sold beer, so we set off, full of hopeful anticipation, to find it. When we found the hotel it was not exactly five, or indeed two, star and was undergoing building works, but the bar was operational around the back. We found the front door to the bar, guarded by two muscled guards, who opened the door for us. We entered a large, sparsely furnished room with sombre and sorry-looking men sat around at cheap tables drinking their beers. No laughter, no music or any enervating buzz of conversation in the room, just gloomy looks and a depressing atmosphere. We ordered two beers and drank them in this sad environment, reminiscent of what I imagine might have been a sleazy Chicago speakeasy during the Great Depression of the thirties.

It was after we discovered that air freighting a new wheel to Casablanca would take at least a week, probably longer with the administration and copious paperwork required by customs, that we began planning our 'Great Escape'. We needed to get to an international airport. There were no internal flights from La Ayoune for a few days, no hire cars, and the only coach available was fully booked. Alistair negotiated, with the assistance of a helpful local policeman, a special deal with a taxi driver to take us to Marrakech, a mere 532 miles north. We set off just after lunch.

Our journey to Marrakech was met with many road checks by the police in Western Sahara and Southern Morocco. Mostly this involved waiting until the taxi was called forward by the police – a quick look in the car and we were waved through. We were asked to get out of the taxi at one road checkpoint, where the gendarme asked the purpose of our journey. The perplexed look on his face was priceless as he listened to Alistair's explanation, which began "Well, the wheel fell off our aeroplane and we were stuck at La Ayoune and ...". With eyes raised to the heavens, he waved us through with an impatient swish of his traffic-directing arm.

Twelve and a half hours later, we arrived at Marrakech to find, by chance, an Ibis Hotel that had spare beds at one o'clock in the morning. Phew! First stage of the escape plan successfully completed, and we did not have to dig a tunnel. Not sure that I am eager to break the record for my longest taxi ride any time soon, however.

After a night's rest, we were able to book seats on an Air France flight to Toulouse and take the commercial flight back to Alistair's Gaillac home. I collected my car from the barn and drove back to England, stopping overnight on the Île d'Oleron.

The recovery of F-PLAN was deferred until December, which allowed Alistair and his wife, Liz, to enjoy their planned one month's holiday in Australia. During November, the engineers at MDS Aviation flew to La Ayoune, fitted the new wheel, and flew F-PLAN back to Casablanca to await our return.

The Postscript

I flew by EasyJet to Toulouse, for the weekend of 8/9 December, where Alistair met me in the terminal building. We had been watching the weather for Morocco and Spain, and a window of clear weather was forecast for early the following week. A pleasant weekend was spent with Alistair and Liz, enjoying life in the south of France and watching Heineken Cup rugby on the television, with English and Welsh clubs taking on French teams from Toulouse, Toulon, and Clermont-Ferrand – without much success as it transpired. Then the Irish Munster side rubbed salt in the wounds by beating Saracens.

Alistair and I caught the morning Air France flight to Casablanca on Monday, where we were met by Aziz from MDS Aviation, who drove us to Tit Mellil, the general aviation airfield in Casablanca. After a lunch at the local equestrian club we went to visit F-PLAN, who was tucked up, nice and warm, in the hangar, looking very smart with her new wheel. It was during our visit to the control tower to discuss our flight to Tangier that we ran into our first logistical problem. King Mohammed VI was visiting Casablanca, and a blanket ban on all aviation was in place, except for scheduled flights into the main airport of Mohammed V.

So until the king decided to move to his next destination, we were stuck here. Bit worrying also, as there was a perfect weather window for the next two days before it all went belly up with cold fronts, occluded fronts – you name them and they were coming! Undaunted, we filed our flight plan and agreed we would be back first thing tomorrow with hopeful looks on our faces.

Alistair had found a clean hotel, with the mandatory requirement of free WiFi, which was only €40 for a twin-bedded room. The Manzil Hotel turned out to be alright, a bit like a small Ibis hotel, but the area of Roche Noire in which it was located left quite a lot to be desired. But hey, we were only here for the one night – we hoped! Not wishing to look for a restaurant in the Roche Noire district, we took a taxi to Rick's Cafe in the hope of meeting Ingrid Bergman or listening to Dooley Wilson play 'As Time Goes By'. Although neither of them were there that evening, or indeed any of the other characters from the film *Casablanca*, we did enjoy an excellent meal in a beautiful courtyard-style house with high curved arches and Moorish architecture.

Our alarms went off at six the next morning and after breakfast we left for Tit Mellil airfield. The tower had good news that the notice to airmen, banning all flights during the king's visit, had been lifted, and we were free to depart. I flew the first leg to Tangiers, lifting off just after nine o'clock and landing an hour and three quarters later on the easterly runway at Tangier. Now on to the next logistical problem: how to get authorisation to leave Morocco.

We had received advice that flights in Morocco required an authorisation number, such as was issued back in October the succinct and snappy code 'No85/DTA/DRTAA/SAGTDA'. We split our resources and I was charged with refuelling the aircraft while Alistair went off to negotiate with customs, police, and air traffic. Thirty minutes later, he returned, all smiles, as he had discovered that the authorisation was only required for flying in the south of Morocco, and we were clear to go.

We departed just after midday, and I remained in the P1 seat for the three hour flight to Murcia in southern Spain. On the advice of the lady at the information desk in the airport terminal, we checked into the Mar Menor Hotel in the seaside resort of Santiago de la Ribera. With our paperwork completed, it was time to start the search for a paella restaurant, which proved unsuccessful, but Alistair did spot a small family-run tapas bar that took up most of our evening, as we sampled their various tasty dishes and local wines.

With the clear weather holding, although cloudy and with occasional stormy showers, Alistair took off just after ten in the morning, with me in the co-pilot seat looking after navigation and radio calls. We climbed to 7,500 feet and found ourselves above the dense cloud layer, with only blue skies above. And so it stayed for the next four hours, and actually improved as we rounded the easterly corner of the Pyrenees, close to Perpignan, where we found that the south of France was enjoying a cloudless and clear blue sky day. In no time at all, we were over Carcassonne and tracking to Gaillac airfield. The air traffic controller at Toulouse agreed to close our flight plan and Alistair executed a textbook landing on the westerly grass runway at Gaillac. We were home.

Two tired and happy pilots had completed the adventure we began more than two months earlier, as the below photo of Alistair aptly demonstrates.

Pierre-George Latécoère being an astute businessman, in addition to an aviation pioneer, spotted a further gap in the market for his Aéropostale service.

In flying from France to the French Colonies in North Africa, his pilots had to fly the length of Spain. Why not collect Spanish mail on the way and deliver to the Spanish colonies? Apart from Spanish Sahara, now know as Western Sahara, squeezed in between Morocco and Mauritania, the rest of Spain's colonies were in South America. Similarly, Portugal had need of a postal service to Brazil. The logistical problem was that there were no aircraft, at the time, with the range necessary to fly across the Atlantic. The problem was solved by flying the mail to Dakar, in Senegal, where the mail could be transported by ship to Natal in the north east corner of Brazil.

Saint Exupéry, among others, was tasked with establishing a network of airfields in Brazil, Uruguay, Argentina, Chile, Paraguay, and Peru. So by 1927, the Aéropostale pilots were collecting mail from Natal and flying south along the eastern coastline of South America, then making the dangerous flight over the Andes mountains to reach the western coastline.

We have a film club in Beaconsfield, with a selection committee that excels in choosing good prize-winning art films that do not make the main cinema chains, as well as delightful old classics.

Last Saturday was one such old classic, the 1939 film, *Only Angels Have Wings*. Cary Grant plays the ace pilot, with Rita Hayworth as the girl he loved and lost and for whom he still 'carries a torch', as the expression goes. The story is about a group of hardened and gung-ho American flyers in the fictitious South American town of Barranca, braving the inclement weather and treacherous mountain passes of the Andes to deliver the mail by air. It's a good tale of heroism and flying skills with excellent aerial photography made before the days of computer-generated special effects.

What I did notice was that all the aircraft in the film had the French 'F' registrations. I began to wonder if this was not really the story of the French Aéropostale pilots in South America that Hollywood had re-cast with American heroes to sell the story to the American public. Of course, I could be wrong.

There are, and have been, many superb US pilots, but I suspect that the film draws heavily on the experiences and lives of Henri Guillaume, Jean Mermoz, Marcel Reine, and Antoine de Saint Exupéry, amongst the many other French pioneering aviators.

For my third story, I join my French friends from Raid Latécoère again, this time with my pilot friend from Denham airfield, Robin Wicks, for another adventure, flying in South America during April and May 2014. This story, entitled "Flying Down to Rio", follows the Aéropostale pilots who established the airmail routes throughout Argentina, Uruguay, and Brazil. My French pilot friend, Isabelle Grimaud, swapped places with Robin for the journey from the north of Brazil back to Uruguay.

Flying Down to Rio
South America
13 April to 31 May 2014

The Journey
Flying Down to Rio

On reflection, I should have noticed that it was unusual to have half a dozen photographers crouching alongside the runway, taking shots of our landing at the Natal Aeroclub. We had seen many unusual sights during our landings as we flew north along the Atlantic coast of Brazil, including a man driving a horse and cart at the opposite end of one runway upon which we had just touched down. The photographers were, however, a first.

As we turned right onto the taxiway, we saw that there were no aircraft in the hangars, which were now full of smartly dressed people milling around tables of food. There seemed to be a party going on. We stopped the engine and, as I opened the door to leave the cockpit, I could hear the sound of an accordion band playing music. The mayor and mayoress of Natal walked towards me and shook my hand warmly, greeting me with "Bienvenue à Natal". It was only then that I realised that we were the honoured guests for whom this celebration was organised and for whom the band was playing. Robin, my good friend and co-pilot, starting chatting initially in French, soon switching to Portuguese as I was whisked away for a television interview, thankfully, in English.

What a way to complete our flying journey, which started at Rio Gallegos in the south of Argentina and had finished in the top right hand corner of Brazil some three weeks later. Being greeted by a seventeen-piece accordion band on landing was definitely a bit special.

This journey really started two years before, when we landed at Dakar in Senegal. That time I was with Alastair Moon on a flying safari, or 'Raid' as the French call it, organised by the Raid Latécoère group, which retraces the steps, or possibly wingtips, of the French Aéropostale pilots of the 1920's and 30's. We had, in 2012, flown from France, through Spain, across the

Straits of Gibraltar to Morocco, then onto Western Sahara and Mauritania before arriving in Senegal, with our stop in Dakar.

As Monsieur Latécoère sought ways to grow his Aéropostale business, he reasoned that both Spain and Portugal had a need for an airmail service to their colonies. Only real problem was, the Atlantic Ocean was in the way of flying to South America. The shortest route was, and still is, from Dakar in Senegal to Natal in Brazil, but that is still 1,450 nautical miles. You can save 200nm by landing on the Fernando de Noronha Islands, but with aircraft that flew 110 knots, assuming no headwinds, that was still anything between 12 and 15 hours of flying.

With no aircraft capable of flying such a distance without refuelling, the Latécoère 28 seaplane was developed with the plan that this could land on the ocean alongside an oil tanker for refuelling and then take off again. With no GPS, flying only with a compass, stopwatch, and calculating wind drift, the pilot then had to find a tiny dot of a ship in the vastness of the Atlantic Ocean – probably twice – before reaching South America. That takes huge skill, a lot of courage, and a large helping of luck. They did it (not without losses of planes and pilots), and the South American Aéropostale was created.

And … that is why I was in Natal.

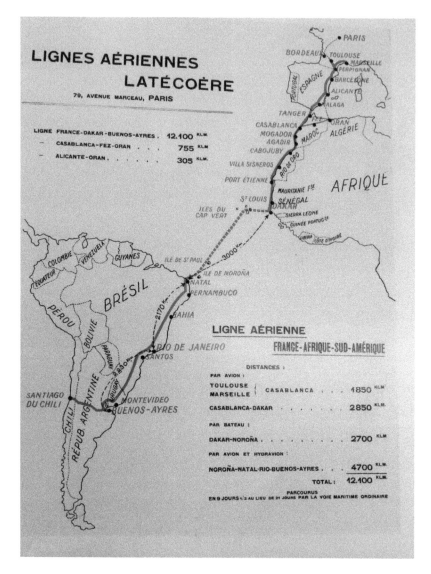

Discovering Patagonia

I had left Heathrow on Sunday 13 July to fly to Buenos Aires with Robin Wicks. We were joining the Raid Latécoère group of French pilots on their flying adventure through Argentina, Uruguay, and Brazil.

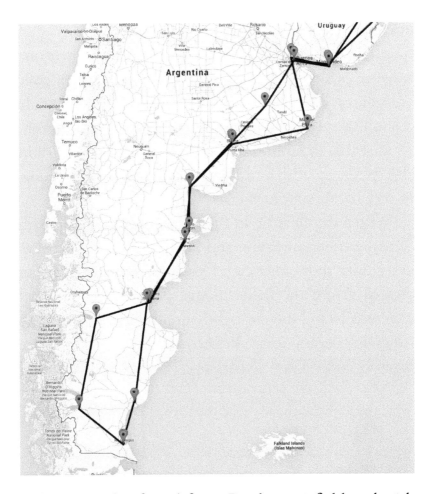

Robin is a pilot friend from Denham airfield and with whom I had flown in Libya in 2009 when Robin piloted his own aircraft, G-IJAG, on that adventure. We would be flying together this time for the next five weeks, sharing the duties both in the cockpit and in the ground preparation of our hired aircraft.

Robin also possesses another invaluable skill, with his linguistic talents. My 'restaurant' French is woefully inadequate to cope with a twenty minute aviation briefing, especially when delivered at machine gun speed. It is, after all, rather important to know where one is flying, which bumps in the landscape might impede one's flight, and which airspace should be avoided while the military are practising firing with live ammunition. As a bonus, in addition to French and German Robin also speaks Spanish and Portuguese, which would come in very handy on our travels.

With a day to spare in Buenos Aires, we met up with Eliana, a friend of Robin and Lety, his wife. Eliana gave us a guided tour of her city; I had a romantic expectation of a city from the Belle Epoque period with beautiful architecture and men in tightly fitted tail coats escorting ladies in elegant long dresses, shouldering white lace parasols. Sadly, I saw no parasols. The nineteenth century

fine buildings were there, looking their age, sadly, and hemmed in with shops, dull houses, and pavements in urgent need of pothole repair work.

It all reflects an Argentina that was once among the richest countries in the world but where the last eighty years of political instability has fostered the gradual decline of its wealth into bankruptcy. The centre of the city has modern tower blocks, smart shopping avenues, wide thoroughfares, and dockside areas of trendy restaurants and expensive blocks of flats with views over the water of the now inoperative Puerto Madero.

The city has a strong history and celebrates its hero General José de San Martin, who is accredited with the liberation of Argentina from Spanish colonial rule. Somewhat more controversial is Julio Argentino Roca, renowned military general and president in the second half of the 1800s. He presided over the growing wealth of the nation, encouraged mass immigration from Europe, but also, more shamefully, drove out and killed the dark-skinned southern settlers that had migrated to Argentina. One seems to see only white faces in Argentina.

The other person who figures prominently is Eva Perón. Her influence is still strong. Her face is displayed widely and one prominent tower block has two large images of her face displayed and visible from the main ten-lane Avenida 9th Julio, which accommodates a permanent traffic jam through the centre of the city. Eliana showed us the balcony from where Eva made speeches to her adoring public. We visited her tomb in the large and impressive cemetery where one still has to queue for a glimpse of Eva's final resting place. One does wonder, however, if the legacy of Eva Perón is part of the problem in Argentina, where only about half of the population  works and creates wealth whilst the other half, the poorer half, has been taught that they should be supported by the state providing for them. So much talent, so much natural resource, which remains dormant through lack of political will, it would seem.

The old port area of La Boca, the 'mouth' of the river Plate, is a colourful area of brightly painted buildings, bustling street cafes, tango dancers, and artists. It was here that I tasted my first of the cone-shaped Havanna chocolates, containing the much loved, and delicious, 'dulce de leche' cream filling. If you taste one, you will definitely want a second one.

The area is home to the Boca Juniors football team, long-time rivals of the other team in Buenos Aires, River Plate. Both originally wanted to wear red shirts as their team colours, so a football match was organised with the winner getting their wish. River Plate won and wear the red. Boca Juniors decided that the colours of the next ship to arrive in the original port would determine the colours of their shirts. The next ship that docked was Swedish, and the blue and yellow colours of its flag were adopted for the shirts of the Boca Juniors players.

The Peso is the currency of Argentina and can only be exchanged in Argentina. External banks and bureaux de change will not trade in pesos because its exchange rate is so volatile. The official exchange rate was between 7 and 8 to the US dollar. Limitations on the availability of foreign currency to Argentineans have led to the development of a 'blue' market, with an exchange rate of 10 to 12 pesos to the dollar. This market is openly traded along the wide Avenida Florida shopping area, where every twenty yards or so one passes street traders, looking slightly shady, calling out "cambio, cambio" from the corners of their mouths. After enquiring and agreeing on their exchange rate, one is escorted into an empty office building or shop, naturally with blinds covering the windows, where notes are exchanged, checked, and pocketed before departing from this walk on the wild side of monetary life in Argentina.

Our aircraft were being hired from Montevideo, the capital city of Uruguay, which is just across the River Plate from Buenos Aires. We decided to use the ferry crossing. The River Plate is a surprisingly wide river and the journey takes three hours, by high speed ferry, to make the 110 mile crossing.

Somewhere, at the bottom of the river, lies the wreck of the German pocket battleship Graf Spee. After the end of the First World War, Germany was prohibited by the Treaty of Versailles from building battleships. It was alright for them to build smaller frigates and cruisers but not the largest capital ships for its naval fleet. The Germans came up with a cunning plan. They would use their engineering brilliance to build a battleship that fitted within the dimensions of the smaller cruiser warship permitted by the treaty but had the destructive power of the full-sized battleship. The result was the 'pocket battleship' of which three were built. See what comes from not having taught the Germans how to play cricket!

The Admiral Graf Spee was completed in 1936 and, after the outbreak of the Second World War, was off the coast of South America, attacking merchant ships trying to deliver much-needed cargo to Great Britain. The British Navy engaged the Graf Spee in the sea Battle of the River Plate but, without the benefit of a battleship, the three lighter cruisers were outgunned and the Ajax and Achilles were severely damaged, with HMS Exeter being put out of action. The Graf Spee sustained some superficial damage and retreated to the neutral port of Montevideo for repairs.

The British Admiralty gave orders for larger ships to sail to Montevideo, but the Graf Spee would be ready to sail out of harbour before they could get to Uruguay. Then followed much subterfuge and cables were sent, containing false information about the imminent arrival of the British fleet, which it was known would be intercepted by the German spy network. The ruse worked, and the Germans, fearing the capture of their pocket battleship, ordered the captain to scuttle the ship in the River Plate. And it is still there today.

At the airfield of Angel S. Adami, in Montevideo, we were taught by instructor Santiago Sosa how to land the Cessna 177 Cardinal that Robin and I would fly in Argentina. Having been signed off as proficient, we celebrated with a large fish lunch and a huge steak dinner.

Friday 18 April, and we set off for our journey through Argentina, with our first flight to Buenos Aires, where we would clear customs. There is a lot of paperwork when flying between countries in South America, to satisfy the requirements of the flight control authorities, customs, immigration, and police. The General Declaration form, or GenDec, is required with details of both the aircraft and the crew. Twelve copies of GenDecs are required, all needing the official stamp. The Uruguayans want five copies, the Argentineans need three copies, but no-one knows who needs the other four copies, but they all know if you don't have them you cannot cross the border!

After dinner in Buenos Aires, Robin took his customary evening walk after a big meal, whilst I crashed into bed. Perhaps I should have kept him company, as I had been charged with the responsibility of looking after him by his wife, Lety. Alone in Buenos Aires, Robin stopped to join a knot of people watching some evening event in Plaza San Martin when he heard a female voice behind him say,

"Hello, how nice to see you again."

Turning around, Robin didn't recognise the lady and said that there must be some mistake, as they had not met before.

"Yes we have," she says. "We met this morning."

"But I was in Montevideo this morning," explains Robin.

"Aah!" says the lady, "my apologies, it must have been someone who looks just like you. No matter, why don't we have a drink anyway?" (*Quick thinking on her part!*)

Robin politely declines, explaining that he had left his wallet in his hotel room. "No matter," she replies, "I can come back to your room to help you look for your wallet"! Time to beat a quick retreat.

We were five aircraft on the journey south in Argentina.

'*Foxtrot Oscar*' with Belgian pilot Alain and his wife Claudine;

'*Golf Kilo*' (later to become infamous) with three pilots, two from Reunion, Joel and Vincent, and Patrick from Alsace;

'*Lima Whisky*' was flown by Arthur Brocas, Jacques, and Michel;

'*Alpha Romeo*' the larger Cessna 206 Stationair, had Carole Descazeaux, joint chief pilot with Arthur, flying with logistics lady Marie-Cecile and photographer

Meliane. The other Jacques made up the crew of four, but as the only man among three females he didn't get too much chance to speak!

Robin and I in '*Hotel Juliet*' were the crew for the fifth aircraft.

Just over four hours flying south over pampas grasslands, ideal for rearing beef cattle, brought us to the beautiful seaside resort of Mar del Plata, where we met up with Argentinean pilots Bruno and Carlos, who would join us on our journey. They would be flying an unusual aircraft, the Cessna 337 Skymaster, which has one propeller on the nose of the aircraft and a second pusher propeller at the rear of the fuselage, between the twin boom tail configuration.

You could believe you're in Biarritz or San Sebastian when driving along the splendid esplanade at Mar del Plata; there are high-rise apartments along the seafront and elegant shops selling luxury goods. We visited the port, where trawlers are huddled together, saw the seals on the rocks, breathed in the salty and fishy aromas, and listened to a chubby Italian-looking accordionist singing 'O Sole Mio'. This was a reminder of the huge influx of Italians among the 12 million immigrants to settle in Argentina in the nineteenth century.

Following the route of the Latécoère pilots, we continued south to Bahia Blanca, where, as guests of the naval airbase, we hangared our planes in the same hangar used by those Aéropostale pilots. We were shown round the Museum of Naval Aviation, and the Falklands War exhibits had pride of place. "This was the radar aircraft that found HMS Sheffield" and "this aircraft was based at Puerto Argentino (as Port Stanley was renamed by the Argentineans)". The Falklands War was probably the biggest event in the history of Argentinean military aviation and they talk about it with huge pride. Indeed, they have reason to be proud of the bravery and achievements of their pilots flying aircraft that, apart from the Super Etendard, were not really a match for the British military aircraft technology, although hearing them talk you would not gain the impression that they came in at second place in the war.

Normally, we land at airfields with petrol-pump-style refuelling facilities, much like filling the fuel tank in one's car but with the one difference of attaching an earth lead to the aircraft to protect against any static electricity spark potentially causing an explosion in the fuel tank. Occasionally, we land at an aeroclub where the fuel tank has no pump. On such an occasion the twenty litre watering can is used, which, when full of avgas, is carried

by hand to the aircraft, where, for a high wing plane, it is carried up the pair of steps to the top of the wing, and poured into a large funnel complete with muslin gauze liner held in place with bulldog clips. Thus, any dirt in the fuel is filtered out and cannot clog the carburettor – avoiding the situation where the engine stops working in mid-air! The first watering can is not too heavy. But for an aircraft requiring 100 litres, it does get very hard work towards the end, especially when there are four more aircraft to be refuelled!

Hotel Juliet is temperamental about starting. Her battery and starter motor do not seem to get on with each other. Sometimes, turning the ignition key just produces a dull whirring sound without the propeller being turned at all. Other times the starter motor engages but after three laboured rotations of the prop it gives up trying. One's hope is that the spark plugs will catch and the engine will fire on the first few turns.

As the temperature cools going south, starting Hotel Juliet became more temperamental. All sorts of waggling and shaking routines were interspersed with various pleadings, mantras, and curses. So far, she has always succumbed to all this cajoling and started, eventually.

Our evening meal was at a Parrillada restaurant, where we ate heartily and were much impressed by Bruno's ability to devour pretty much one side of a barbecued beef cow. Much red wine later, unwisely topped off with the restaurant's homemade limoncello, we slept, and snored, very soundly.

In rather fewer numbers than the Italian immigrants, colonies of Welsh settlers came to Argentina. We visited Puerto Madryn and Trelew (Lewis Town) with the temperature dropping noticeably from northern Argentina. Sadly for the Welsh immigrants wishing to establish Welsh settlements to protect their language and customs they felt were being eroded in the Industrial Revolution at home, they arrived in Patagonia, where the lush green pampas is replaced by barren rocky ground and little fresh water. They survived in these harsh conditions and helped build the railway system, among other activities. Evidence of the Welsh presence is hard to find today, although it still exists.

Trelew has an atmospheric cafe set within the Hotel Touring Club. The place was built in 1898 and looks little changed from when pilots Antoine de Saint Exupéry and Jean Mermoz, amongst others, ate and slept there. Whilst the Latécoère pilots are remembered, the greater emphasis seems to be on the visit of Butch Cassidy and the Sundance Kid whilst on the run from US law officers.

So cold was it the following morning that the starter motor of our aircraft refused to turn the propeller, despite all the tried and tested black magic spells and mechanical massage tricks. Luckily, Pablo, from the local flying club, was around and, familiar with this problem, hand swung the prop to kick our engine into life. I remember chuckling when I found out that Robin had packed thermal gloves and a woolly hat for our trip to South America. I was not laughing now, and Robin had that self-satisfied 'I told you so' look on his face as I shivered in the cold morning air.

So, seven days after leaving Montevideo, and after seventeen hours of flying, we landed at Rio Gallegos, level with the Falkland Islands, which was our southerly destination on this trip. Two rest days were scheduled and both Robin and I felt this was much deserved and needed to recharge our batteries for the long return trip north.

Two of the crews were leaving at Rio Gallegos, or shortly thereafter, and wished to top off their adventure with a further flight south to Ushuaia, the capital of Tierra del Fuego and the most southerly city in Argentina, some say the world. Our aircraft didn't have the range to do the journey, and we were in any case in need of a rest, so Robin and I opted to stay.

After a shopping trip to buy my thermal gloves and a woolly hat – and wishing Robin would get that silly smile off his face – we made the ten minute flight to the Rio Gallegos flying club. We met Ricardo Hermida, the young and charming secretary and flying instructor of the flying club at Rio Chico airfield. I guess we should not have been surprised to find the French Aéropostale hangar and pilot's cottage on the airfield. We keep tripping over the footsteps of these intrepid pilots. This hangar was the second one built for the Aéropostale service in Argentina, the first being the one we used for our aircraft in Bahia Blanca.

Friday was very windy – there is quite a lot of wind in that part of the world! We had accepted Ricardo's kind offer to take us flying that day, and flying we went, despite the fact that the strong wind was across the runway. We flew inland first to see a lake in a mountain-top depression, before returning to the coast to see the old shipwreck in the harbour. Returning to the field, our flying skills were tested as we crabbed sideways on final approach, before firmly kicking the rudder pedal right to bring the aircraft nose in line with the runway at six feet off the ground – might have been five feet, but it worked!

We said goodbye to Alain and Claudine, as well as Arthur, who were all returning home from Rio Gallegos. We were joined by Hervé Berardi, president of Raid Latécoère, Séverine, who worked with Hervé's wife Helene, both being air traffic controllers in the south of France. Séverine, together with the other new arrival, Thierry, would take over the flying of Foxtrot Oscar.

Perito Moreno is probably the best known of the forty-seven large glaciers in the Parque National Los Glaciares, home to a giant ice cap that feeds the glaciers in the southern Andes mountain range. Some of the glaciers flow into Chile, whilst the rest travel in Argentina. Perito Moreno flows into Lago Argentino, just outside the town of El Calafate, and that is where we were headed on leaving Rio Gallegos.

Having flown south following the coastline, our plan for the return journey was to fly inland alongside the Andes mountain range that runs from top to bottom, like a spine separating Argentina from Chile. With all five aircraft repositioned to the aeroclub at Rio Chico, we bade goodbye to Ricardo and friends and flew north west across barren terrain that rose as we got close to the mountains.

From 4,500 feet above the foothills we could see Lake Argentino, with its turquoise green water shining in the sunlight and a backdrop of snow-covered mountains on the far side. To protect the glacier, aircraft are not permitted to overfly but are allowed to fly 25 miles out of the town for a great view from the air before returning over the lake and landing on the easterly runway at El Calafate. Do stay at the Tehuel Plaza hotel should you make a visit to El Calafate. It is a comfortable hotel without being super luxurious, but from its position on a hilltop it has the most magnificent view of the lake and mountains. Worth it just for that view.

The next day was very windy, which is to be expected in Patagonia. Together with the additional turbulence from the nearby mountains it makes for 'sporty' flying. We were first to depart in Hotel Juliet, as Golf Kilo was having problems starting her engine.

Our first stop was at the airfield of Lago Buenos Aires to refuel, where the wind was a blustery 30 knots gusting to 40. That would have been challenging on its own but to this was added the problem that there was no airfield at the GPS location provided to us. After twenty minutes of flying around and searching the ground, we decided to contact an adjacent airfield on the radio and were given a heading that took us ten kilometres away from where we were looking! At last we saw the gravel runway, made radio calls to pass the correct coordinates to our friends in the following aircraft, and made the tricky landing.

Eventually, the aircraft following us appeared, landed, and refuelled, but there was no sign of Golf Kilo. We learned that they did get the engine started but on the journey it started to experience rough running. It is probably worth saying that most aircraft systems are duplicated to provide a backup in the event that one component fails in the air. This is exactly what happened to Golf Kilo. After various checks, the crew discovered that the left magneto was providing no spark for the plugs and they were reliant only on the right magneto. Not an ideal situation, and it explained why they were having difficulty starting Golf Kilo that morning. The decision was made to divert to the coastal airfield of Comodoro Rivadavia, where engineering facilities were available. So our planned route north was cancelled and we would miss out on the Andes and visiting Esquale and Bariloche.

We departed and headed back to the coast to join Golf Kilo. The wind was still blowing hard but, fortunately, straight down the runway at Comodoro, where on approach we had an air speed of 100 knots but were slowed by the headwind to only 50 knots speed over the ground. It seemed to take ages to reach the runway for the landing.

The following day, we flew on to Trelew for refuelling before our night stop in Puerto Madryn. Golf Kilo remained at Comodoro, awaiting fitting of a new magneto. Lima Whisky was in fine form, but during its visit to Ushuaia the aircraft documents mysteriously disappeared. These are the aircraft's passport papers and required to be shown to the police at the larger airports. So not only were Joel, Patrick, and Vincent waiting for a new magneto for their aircraft, but Jacques and Michel had to leave their aircraft at Trelew as they would have been inspected – and found wanting – at Puerto Madryn.

As a result, only Robin and I in Hotel Juliet and Hervé and Séverine in Foxtrot Oscar flew to Puerto Madryn, while Jacques and Michel took a taxi from Trelew – luckily not too far away. So it was just the six of us that went out for an excellent evening meal in Puerto Madryn, where we enjoyed flambé panqueque manzana for dessert. Great fun. Carole and her crew, together with Bruno and Carlos, remained with the stricken Golf Kilo in Comodoro.

The new left magneto was fitted in Golf Kilo, and worked fine, but it was somewhat unnerving for the pilots to discover that twenty minutes into its flight from Comodoro, the right magneto, which hitherto had been the only one working, failed. What, they wondered, would have happened had both magnetos failed at the same time when flying over the foothills of the Andes? Joel, Vincent, and Patrick had by now lost confidence in the aircraft – and who can blame them? Who wouldn't have been spooked by that? So the following day it was decided to leave Golf Kilo behind until it was comprehensively overhauled and proven safe to fly. As if by fate, Vincent and Joel had planned to return home at the mid-point of the flight north. Were they so indiscreet as to mention this to Golf Kilo, who took umbrage, I wonder? So it was commercial flights and farewell to our friends from the Indian Ocean island of Reunion.

Our next stop north was Bahia Blanca, where we were all reunited, albeit with one aircraft missing, at El Mundo Parilla for a meal of Argentinean grilled meats and Mendoza red wine. Ate too much again!

The weather had been kind to us while in Argentina, but today was different, with thick cloud for the second half of our journey to Olivarria and thereon back to Buenos Aires. We were able to fly in the clear blue sky

above the cloud layer for most of the journey. This is a lovely way to fly, with clear visibility and smooth air, unlike the murk and bumpy air below the cloud layer.

Only problem is how to get back down through the clouds when you are nearing the destination airfield. So from forty to fifty miles out, one is looking for a big hole in the clouds to allow a descent. The aircraft ahead found a hole and radioed its location but by the time we arrived at the spot, the hole had closed up again. So they were under the clouds and we were above, separated by a seemingly solid blanket of cloud. Various hoped for holes were spotted ahead but turned out to be 'tricks of the light' until we finally saw our escape route and down we went.

For the second half of our day's flying into Buenos Aires we stayed under the cloud all the way! Bumpy but less stressful.

For some reason, Argentinean taxis are very small. Think Fiat Cinquecento and you won't be too far wrong. True, they can carry four passengers, but that means three are squashed into the back seat. The technique is the biggest person sits beside the driver and the thinnest passenger sits in the middle of the back row. I never seemed to sit in the middle seat! Bigger problems arise when the passengers also have luggage, which invariably caused a look of surprise mixed with bewilderment on the face of the taxi driver. On opening the microscopic boot, one discovers that two thirds of the space is taken up by the LPG tank and the rest of the space contains a bucket full of sponges, a collection of cardboard boxes, and a pair of boots. There is no way that four suitcases will fit in. What can be shoehorned in the space is and the rest goes on your laps. Then, at the end of this ride, you get to pay for the experience too!

The motto for flying trips is 'Hurry up and wait'. Every day you have an early start and inevitably something contrives to have you waiting and waiting and waiting at the airfield. The day of our flight back to Montevideo was no exception, with a 0645 departure from the hotel, missing the breakfast, which didn't start until 0730. Further delays ensued, with taxis whose drivers didn't know where the airfield was and a painful meeting with 'Mr. Jobsworth', who wished to see every piece of paper that one could conceivably imagine.

At last we were ready, aircraft checked, and a gin clear day to fly, when word came from the meteorological office that the visibility was only 2000 meters and we were prohibited from taking off. Pointing out that we could see for miles in this clear air had little effect as we waited for the next forecast bulletin, due in forty minutes, when the forecasters caught up with the reality outside of their cosy office, where they sat analysing their computer data, and where looking out the window is regarded as cheating!

Suffice to say, we did get back to Montevideo, but rather later than planned.

Uruguay

We were back in Adami Airport in Montevideo and there was much to do. Having flown from Argentina, we had to unload all our luggage from our aircraft for customs inspection and complete the forms required by the immigration lady, who listened to classical music while she worked slowly and meticulously through the paperwork and we had our passports checked by the police. Our aircraft needed to be returned to the hangars for engineering maintenance – except for Golf Kilo which was still languishing in Comodoro – and bills needed to be paid. It took forever!

The planning then began for Brazil, where we would be just two aircraft. Alpha Romeo, the Cessna 206, was scheduled to be on the journey, but it had developed a nasty habit of burning oil, which was now at the unsustainable rate of one litre per hour of flight. A new aircraft was located, a twin-engined Piper Seneca CX-BMJ, with six seats. This was to be the sky chariot for Hervé, Carole, Marie-Cecile, Meliane, and Séverine, so Hervé would be heavily outnumbered in this otherwise all-female crew.

Robin and I changed Hotel Juliet, which was too slow for the long flights in Brazil. We inherited the Cessna 182, CX-BLW, whose registration was easily remembered by the mnemonic 'Boys Like Whisky'! Lima Whisky, as she was more correctly known, flew twenty to thirty knots faster than old Hotel Juliet, had the unusual feature that nearly all the instruments in the cockpit worked, and had new papers just arrived from DINACIA, the Uruguayan Aviation Authority, that made the aircraft legal again. Robin and I were very happy.

We had the afternoon and evening in Montevideo, which is small for a capital city, but then Uruguay is not a large country and only has a population of three and a quarter million. That's about the same number of people that live in Berlin or, say, Madrid.

Montevideo has charm but sightseeing did not take too long. As in Argentina, the population were very fond of their caffeine-rich drink called Mate, pronounced 'mat-ay'. The leaves of the yerba mate are dried and chopped, similar to tea leaves, and then steeped in hot water. The drink is held in a hollow calabash gourd, sometimes with ornamented carving or with a silver metal rim. A straw, traditionally made of silver, is used to drink the mate, acting as a filter for the liquid, which is seemingly full of floating leaves. People walk around their offices and along the street carrying their gourds and sipping the mate through the metal straw. Since the drink can be replenished with hot water, the other essential component is a thermos flask of hot water, usually tucked under one arm. Mate drinkers ideally need three arms should they wish to shake hands with friends or carry shopping bags or a briefcase in addition to their thermos and mate gourd.

Saturday morning, 3 May, we departed for the north of Uruguay for a stop in Melo. Our departure was delayed by the lovely gesture of Fernando, the airport manager, who had bought us a chocolate cake with three candles to celebrate the third year of visits by the Raid Latécoère

Group. We flew one hundred and eighty nautical miles north, landing just before sunset at 1730. Sunset is very early in that part of the world, with it being dark by six in the evening. By the time we got to our hotel, the storm clouds that were in the west had arrived, dumping heavy rain accompanied by thunder and lightning. We decided to eat in at the hotel that night!

The weather did not look good on Sunday morning. The warm front had settled over the town with a cloud base of less than 500 feet. We had been cleared by the customs lady to leave for Brazil, so we spent the day in the tiny airport looking at the sky, which remained resolutely grey and overcast. The welcoming committee, local press reporters, and photographers awaiting us at Pelotas in Brazil were as frustrated as we were. All of our flights were under visual flight rules in South America, and in those circumstances it was the weather that decided when we could fly.

The hotel was surprised to see us back again that evening. There were rooms for us but the restaurant was closed on Sunday. Marie-Cecile organised a take-away picnic in the hotel lobby, and the helpful receptionist opened the bar and, after a few beers, things did not seem quite so bad.

On Monday we got ready to make another attempt to leave Uruguay for Pelotas. The weather was still gloomy in the morning, but the afternoon forecast contained signs of hope. We met the customs lady again, who simply changed the dates on the exit stamps in our passports. How pragmatic is that? Sure enough, the clouds started to thin and become fluffy and friendly, so we could depart just after midday, fly above the clouds, and arrive in Pelotas an hour later.

There's an Awful Lot of Coffee in Brazil

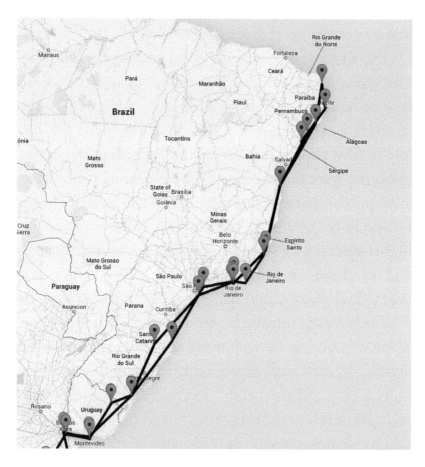

...but the funny thing is that it is really difficult to get a good cup of coffee anywhere in the country. Most places just serve the sort of coffee that you find in those glass flasks that have been sitting over a low light for two hours and certainly don't taste like proper coffee. Best coffee I tasted was in the Coffee Museum, of which more later. I guess all the good stuff is exported and the poor old Brazilians are left with the coffee no-one else wants.

My pilot's licence permits me to fly my UK aircraft anywhere in the world, which in reality means anywhere in Europe and North Africa. Any further than that and it is easier to fly to the country by commercial airline and hire a plane from that country. Only snag is that I then need to have a licence issued by that country to fly the hired plane. Usually this involves taking an Air Law exam and providing enough paperwork to fill a small van, then waiting while the country's civil servants, running that country's aviation authority, issue a licence. This is not regarded as worth turning into a 'rush job' – unless three months constitutes a rush job in civil service land. Thinking about it, it probably does!

So planning ahead is the mantra for overseas flying. Over the years I have had licences from South Africa, Namibia, Australia, New Zealand, Canada, USA, and now Uruguay. To obtain the Uruguayan licence, we met in Paris back in March, where the French had arranged for an official from DINACIA (or Dirección Nacional de Aviación Civil e Infraestructura Aeronáutica, to its friends), the Uruguayan civil aviation authority, to fly to Paris and conduct the examination. Robin and I joined other pilots from France to sit the multiple choice exam for which we had studied numerous old exam papers and correct answers as preparation. Luckily we did not have to take the exam in Spanish but English, although I am not sure the French pilots regarded this as a very lucky break. Suffice to say we both passed, and Uruguayan licences awaited us on arrival in Montevideo.

Flying in Brazil has an extra paperwork problem, as we also need a document from AVANAC (you guessed it, 'Autorização de Vôo da Agência Nacional de Aviação Civil. Pretty obvious really). Now this document requires information both about the aircraft you will fly in Brazil and also the pilot, and when issued has a unique identification number that must be quoted on all flight plans. In Brazil, one needs a flight plan for every flight, even if all you are doing is taking off, flying in a circle, and landing again at the same place. Obtaining this AVANAC form, and its essential number, was one of the 'simple' bits of administration to be completed at Pelotas, our entry point into Brazil. Ha ha ha!!

Meanwhile, we could enjoy our warm welcome in Pelotas, where we were well looked after by the deputy mayor, Paula Schild Mascarenhas, who was a lecturer of French at the local university, so spoke beautiful French although, sadly for me, no English. After our reception at the town hall and speeches of welcome, we were taken to lunch at the delightful and old fashioned Café Aquários in Rua Quinze de Novembro. Historically a place where the men of the town would gather for coffee, a game of chess, and conversation, it retains its simple wooden tables, marble counters, half-tiled walls, and serves simple but well-cooked food, and alcoholic drinks as well as tea and coffee. It also retains a system where a lady cashier sits in her booth and is responsible for collecting money, running a ticket system that I never fully understood. But the atmosphere is welcoming and comfortable, like putting on a favourite jacket, and you feel you will see an old friend walk through the doors at any moment.

Opposite the town hall was a mercado in a covered market arcade, which had a miniature Eiffel Tower on its roof. French influence seemed to be everywhere in Brazil. Set out in one of the wide walkways between the shops was an exhibition celebrating the achievements of the Latécoère pilots and the airmail business they created in South America.

Black and white photographs, some in sepia tones, were displayed in the exhibition, with text explaining the exploits, history, and routes for the service. One photograph showed an open cockpit biplane flying over

the snow-covered Andes, delivering mail to Chile. Not surprisingly, the pilot was wearing a large leather coat, flying helmet, goggles, and large gauntlets.

On Friday 13 June 1930, Henri Guillaumet was making his 92nd flight over the Andes when bad weather

precipitated a forced landing amongst the snowy peaks near Laguna Diamante. Out of range of any radio message, he walked for one week over three mountain passes before being rescued at dawn on 19 June by a fourteen-year-old boy and taken to the nearby village to recuperate. His single-engine Potez 25 biplane is probably still up in the Andes, somewhere in the mountains. Guillaumet's words, recorded by Saint Exupéry, were "What I have done, I swear, no beast could have done it". The story is told in the movie *Wings of Courage*.

Tuesday was a waiting day. We waited for AVANAC officials, beavering away in Brasilia, to issue our forms and numbers so we might fly north in Brazil. The spelling of my name was corrected from 'Dereck Allway' – or else despite having my passport number and pilot licence number and address and date of birth, how would they know I was not an impostor? Then late that afternoon the 'magic' numbers arrived, but too late to fly that day. I was now allocated AVANAC 0461N14, a number that I would learn by heart, and tomorrow morning we could be on our way.

The weather was alright on Wednesday morning, albeit a bit cloudy. We had two flights to make that day so we could catch up with our planned schedule. First we would fly to Florianópolis for the delayed meeting with the mayor, speeches, and exchange of gifts, after which we'd head on to Santos. Not all schedules go to plan, and as we flew to the north east above the clouds, noticing that they were getting thicker, we heard on the radio that Florianópolis had closed its airport for visual landings. The mayor went back to his office, for the second time in two days, and we diverted inland to the mountain airfield of Lages at 3,064 feet above sea level.

We refuelled, and ate a banana for lunch, before returning to the coastline and flying at 800 feet below the clouds, over the sea in poor visibility. Robin did try a descent to 500 feet, which had slightly better visibility, but then had to climb back up to 800 feet when we needed to fly over the tower blocks built on the promontory, which sat like a long tongue of land reaching out into the ocean. The air force base at Santos was not easy to see in the gloom until we followed the winding river around the docks and found we were lined up on runway 35 for our touchdown at 1650 hours.

Once the aircraft were secured for the night, and we had avoided the neat piles of poo nuggets left by the local capybaras, we were taken by launch across the dirty harbour of Santos port to the ferry terminal on the mainland, where we were met by two guides from the local tourist bureau.

A curious piece of planning had resulted in a major freight train line running along the dockside between the town and the ferry terminal, which was used by commuters on foot and cycle to travel to and from work. A game of chicken became the natural order of commuter life, as people broke into a run or pedalled faster to cross the railway lines inches in front of the slowly advancing locomotive, rather than waiting and missing the next ferry while thirty goods trucks were hauled slowly over the crossing with the locomotive sounding its foghorn repeatedly. The system works; it can be a touch nerve-wracking, and long may it last. Brazilians do not know how lucky they are not to be members of the EU and have Brussels appoint an enthusiastic 'health and safety' official to spoil the fun and make life unbearable for everyone.

Santos is famous for many things, I am sure, but especially as the place where Edson Arantes do Nascimento, better known as Pele, played the vast majority of his football career with the Santos team. Also in Santos is the Coffee Museum, located in a fabulous building with stone columns, marble floors, and an ornate ceiling of stained glass covering the old coffee auction chamber with its carved wooden seats arranged around the bidding floor. Here they serve excellent coffee made to your order. My favourite was the Chapadão de Ferro coffee. We had been brought here by Monika, a woman who is a powerhouse of energy, holds a doctorate in French, and is an enthusiastic researcher of all things Latécoère. She was responsible for the exhibition of Aéropostale photographs and memorabilia that had been set out in the Coffee Museum. Time again for speeches, exchange of gifts, and shaking a lot of hands.

The following morning, we visited the original airfield of Santos used by the Latécoère Aéropostale organisation. The unloved grass field is no longer an airfield, but we met pilots who used to fly there using the 17-35 runway that ran towards to sea. Euclides, a retired airline pilot from VARIG, flew his first solo from this field in a yellow Paulistinha tail dragger, a Brazilian aircraft rather similar to the Piper Cub. He brought along a painting by Coelho, his instructor, recording this memorable event, which no pilot ever forgets.

Sitting under the shade of a large tree, on a simple wooden bench which had sheets of cardboard for a cushion

and backrest upholstery, was a dignified old man wearing a white Panama hat and holding a photo album on his lap. At ninety-one years old he was lucid and alert as he recalled flying from this field as a five-year-old boy in a plane piloted by the legendary Antoine de Saint Exupéry. It transpires that Saint Exupéry had met this man's mother and invited her to accompany him on a flight. We imagined that the handsome and aristocratic Saint Exupéry was a bit surprised when the pretty girl he had chatted up earlier arrived with her five-year-old son to come along for the flight!

The photo album contained small monochrome photos of the event and the airfield of days now past. It is hoped to preserve the airfield by building a museum and returning the runway to its former condition, although the trees and buildings that have built up around the field will preclude its use for flying again.

I had never been to Rio. I had never been to South America either, which could be the reason. But today we were the guests of the Brazilian Airforce at Campo Del Jardim de Matos airfield, home to their Santos Dumont

Museum in Rio de Janeiro. It was misty at first, but the weather improved as we flew into what must be one of the world's most beautiful harbours, with the statue of Christ the Redeemer gazing down on our little aircraft as we flew past Corcovado.

We were met by the brigadier, who was the commanding officer, at the airforce base. After some words of welcome, we attended a short ceremony where a guard of honour placed a bouquet of flowers at the base of the memorial stone and plaque to the famous French aviator, Jean Mermoz. Then the brigadier escorted us around his aviation museum, which was as fine as any museum of aircraft I have seen around the world. I had not realised that the Brazilian Air Force were involved in the Second World War, particularly in Italy. This was also the first time I had seen a replica of the 14-bis aircraft or 'Oiseau de Proie', the 'Bird of Prey'.

Orville and Wilbur Wright are acknowledged to have made the first controlled, powered flight in a heavier-than-air flying machine on December 17, 1903. Five people witnessed those first three flights at Kill Devil Hills, just outside Kittyhawk in North Carolina, including one of the three coastguards, who took a photo of the historic event. The brothers' skill was developing three-axis aircraft controls that enabled the pilot to steer the aircraft and maintain its equilibrium – albeit not for long; twelve seconds for the first flight. The engine used by the Wright Brothers had insufficient power to lift the aircraft into the air

from the ground, so the plane was launched on rails using an external force, namely a large falling weight, to catapult the 'Flyer' into the air.

The honour of being the first man to build an aircraft capable of taking off under its own power goes to Santos Dumont, a Brazilian with a French father. Born and brought up in Brazil, he moved to Paris at the age of 17, where he studied engineering and became fascinated with flying, initially with controllable balloons, or dirigibles, then later building his 14-bis aircraft. He was 33 by the time he claimed the prize for the first flight, piloting his 14-bis aircraft, which flew backwards – that is tail first – in front of a large crowd in Paris on 23 October 1906, officially observed by the Aéro-Club de France.

Debate continues as to who was really first to fly a fixed wing aircraft, but suffice it to say both contenders deserve much praise and credit. Santos Dumont returned to live in Brazil and is a folk hero, with his name appearing all over the country.

On Friday 9 May we headed to Petropolis, a two hour coach ride into the mountains behind Rio, to see the summer house of Santos Dumont. Petropolis is a pretty place, set at 2,800 feet above sea level, surrounded by rich green vegetation and brightly coloured blooms, and much favoured by the artistic community.

The house of Santos Dumont is like something from a fairy tale, painted white with green shutters and a red roof. It is in the town but perched on a hillside. You have to look up to see it from the street and climb steep wooden steps to reach the ground floor. It should really be floating on a cloud, where it would not look at all out of place. It is small. In fact, Santos Dumont revelled in his own design for a minimalist building, where no space was wasted. It is on three floors with an observatory on the roof. He had no need for a kitchen, as the Palace Hotel was on the opposite side of the road and he would make a phone call to order his meals to be delivered.

By now it will come as no surprise to you that from the house, we went to an official reception where we were introduced to another mayor, listened to more speeches, exchanged gifts, and shook more hands. I had no idea how tiring it is being a celebrity. It has its positive side too, as we were taken to a delightful restaurant for a splendid meal, although Marie-Cecile was somewhat surprised when, over coffee, she was awarded the honour of paying for the meal and wine enjoyed by our host, the mayor, and his ten guests. Fame, they say, comes at a price!

We stayed overnight in Petropolis at the house once owned by another Latécoère pilot, Marcel Reine. Yet another dashingly handsome chap who seemed forever surrounded by beautiful women in the photos. I wonder where my pilot training has gone wrong?

This house is now owned by Jose Augusto Wanderley who, whilst charming, did seem to have a fixation with the Little Prince character from the book by Saint Exupéry. The walls were covered with paintings of the little chap, the napkins had the 'Little Prince' embroidered on them, the towels likewise. The plates and dishes were painted with his image, while models of the character, his plane, and other illustrations from the books were on the shelves as ornaments, so it came as no surprise, when I lay my head down to sleep that night, that there he was again on my pillowcase. Enthusiast, collector, or obsessive behaviour?

Cristo Redentor has to be one of the most iconic monuments, standing with its arms outstretched atop the mountain overlooking the bay of Rio de Janeiro. The Art Deco statue has been gazing down on the people of Rio since 1931, and we were off to stand next to it. The taxi can only take you to the mountain railway station in Rua Cosme Velho, from where the red train climbs 2,200 feet above sea level to the top of Corcovado, using a cog wheel track. There was a two hour wait for the next train with space for us, so we opted to use the alternate minibus service, which was excellent. The bus stopped halfway up the mountain so we could enjoy a viewpoint over the bay, before changing to a second bus to the top.

Then a ride in the lift and an escalator later and we were at the foot of Christ the Redeemer, which towered one

hundred feet above us. Without a doubt it is impressive and well worth the journey. We didn't exactly have the place to ourselves, but we managed the obligatory photos and drank in the view over the bay.

As we were now on a sightseeing roll, the next stop was to Pão de Açúcar, better known to us as Sugar Loaf mountain. Two cable cars make the journey to the top, with the intermediate station atop Morro da Urca, where we stopped for a lunchtime beer and empanadas. Although not as high as Corcovado it has such a distinctive shape, and the views from the top are just as breathtaking. You can see the beaches of Copacabana and Ipanema as well as a clear view of Santos Dumont airfield, which seems to float in the bay. Aircraft taking off from this airport fly straight towards Sugar Loaf so employ a steep climbing turn to the left as they depart. With the wind in the other direction, you can watch the commercial traffic fly alongside your viewing platform before making a ninety degree left turn for finals on the north-south runway.

I wore my Copacabana T shirt when we visited the beach, but my shirt was from Copacabana Australia, the existence of which the concierge at our hotel had no idea. So I had my photo taken on Copacabana beach, Rio de Janeiro, wearing my Copacabana shirt from Australia, to send to Louise and Paul and my Australian family. How corny is that? The one disappointment was, as it was late autumn in Rio, the beach was not heaving with beautiful women wearing minimalist bikinis that allow full display of their shapely bottoms. I did spot one in the distance, slightly out of focus when my camera was on full zoom though. Lots of men's beach volleyball in progress, as well as others honing their footballing skills.

The sky was blue and the visibility crystal clear for our departure the following day. We requested, and were granted after much coordination by the air traffic controllers, a transit across the bay, flying past Corcavado, Santos Dumont airfield, and Sugar Loaf Mountain, as well as the many rocky islands that are covered in dark green trees and bushes. Such a privilege and stunning sights. We were on our way north to the smart holiday resort of Vitória, where we landed just before a rainstorm hit the field. We ate that evening at a Churasco restaurant where the grilled beef is brought to your table impaled on a sword and slices are cut for your plate, without limit except for the size of your stomach.

The surprising thing about Brazil is you go to towns that you have never heard of and they turn out to be big cities with skyscrapers. I guess with over two hundred million people in the country one should not really be surprised. But we saw Ilhéus, Aracaju, and Recife, and were surprised by each one.

One exception was Penedo, and we would not have gone there had we not been forced to divert because the weather in Recife had closed the airfield. We knew nothing about Penedo except that it was shown on the map and had a small airfield – and 'small' was the operative word. Once we had found it, and that was not a given, it turned out to be a narrow, short runway in the middle of nowhere. I lined up on finals and about fifty yards before touching down we spotted a teenager riding a bicycle pull out of the bushes onto the runway just ahead of us. He was pedalling furiously as he intended to race us down the runway riding parallel to our aircraft, on a runway only just about wide enough for us! Full power, stick back, and we climb sharply for a go-around circuit. As we come onto finals for the second time there is no sign of the kid on the runway, but we did spot a group of them waiting on the parking apron. It was just as we sighed in relief at landing without incident that we spotted the horse and cart being driven slowly at the far end of the runway!

All in all, a more eventful than usual arrival. It transpired that this was an emergency runway used by the Bomberos, an army unit of firemen. For the village kids, the runway was a playground, and for the horse and cart it was a shortcut. The arrival of our two aircraft was a major event in their lives and in the airfield's logbook. Luckily, the army boys had WiFi, so we could check the weather, confirm that Recife was still shut, and re-route to Aracaju for the night.

I can't remember where we first discovered caipirinhas, but it was a great discovery as it soon became our automatic pre-dinner cocktail. Caipirinha is made from the clear cachaça liqueur, itself made from sugar cane. In Portugal it is known as aguardente, which on its own is a delicious digestif drink, a wise precaution so one is not kept awake at night with indigestion – well, that's my rationale. In Brazil, caipirinha is an aperitif long drink made with lime crushed together with sugar. Add lots of ice, then drown with a generous helping of cachaça and serve with a short straw. Delicious, definitely addictive, and not to be missed.

CAVOK is the aviation code for Ceiling and Visibility OK or, in other words, 'a lovely day for flying'. We had CAVOK for Recife but here in Aracaju and at Maceió en-route it was cloudy, stormy, and the visibility was poor. And so, not for the first time, we sat at the airfield and waited, hoping for an improved weather forecast. The weather was forecast to improve by 3pm, but with a two hour flight to Recife and sunset at 5.08pm, there was no room for delay or alternative plans should Recife get weathered in. Finally, at 2pm, the weather starts to clear, only for us to have a further delay while our expired flight plans need to be refiled.

The advice given to Arthur Dent in *Hitchhikers Guide to the Galaxy* was 'Don't Panic. Always know where your towel is', and much the same applies to pilots – although the towel bit is an optional extra. So we didn't panic, and got away at twenty to three in the afternoon, spending the two hour flight weaving around clouds and rain cells, sometimes on the coast, then tracking inland and finally being asked to orbit until commercial traffic had landed at Recife, before we raced a tropical rainstorm to the airfield. We won the race and our prize was a brilliant rainbow that touched the earth close to the runway upon which we were landing.

The rain arrived shortly after us and did not stop all evening, so that the streets were running with water. Our restaurant that evening had deployed a wooden bridge walkway from the street so we could step out of the taxi onto the wooden slats and cross the street river to get to the restaurant and our table.

Recife was once a key hub in the seventies and eighties for the BOAC and British Caledonian flights to South America. With aircraft that did not have the range to fly non-stop from London to Rio or Buenos Aires, the first South American landfall was at Recife for refuelling and overnight accommodation before the onward flights. Later, when aircraft were developed with the range for the thirteen hour journeys, Recife airfield was consigned to the Transatlantic backwater and survives to serve South and North American flights and as a domestic airfield.

Thursday 15 May was our arrival in Natal, with the aforementioned unexpected welcome. It was here that we had two days rest and a change of aircrews. Robin departed for England and business meetings, and Hervé returned to France to fly the ATR passenger turbo-prop. Séverine returned to her children and her air traffic controller job, and Marie-Cecile was off to her home in France.

Getting the aircraft back to Uruguay

In reality, our journey was done. We had set off to travel the routes of the aviation pioneers of the French Aéropostale service in South America, finishing at Natal. It had been a great trip, we had met a lot of mayors, attended many receptions, seen the Latécoère exhibition in different cities, listened dutifully to speeches in Portuguese that

Henri Guillaumet

only Robin understood, and flown with the ghosts of Pierre-Georges Latécoère, Didier Daurat, Paul Vachet, Antoine de Saint Exupéry, Henri Guillaumet, Jean Mermoz, Marcel Reine, and other courageous pilots from the twenties and thirties. But now it was done. The crews

Antoine de Saint Exupéry

had departed for home, leaving Carole and myself to fly the two aircraft back to Montevideo.

Help was at hand, however, as we were joined by friends to help us with the flying and make the return trip a fun and happy experience.

Carole was joined by three French pilots – Sylvain Lemoine, Alaine Arette and Olivier Kaps – to fly Mike Juliet. I had met Sylvain and Alain on the Senegal trip two years ago, where I had also first met Hervé, Carole, and Arthur. Helping me fly Lima Whisky was my friend from Reunion, Isabelle Grimaud. We had flown together in Namibia, South Africa, Morocco, and around Europe, so this was a friend in need, indeed, glad to have her arriving to share the flying. I did not know that Dominique Lejeune Cressend was also coming along, so that was a lovely surprise, as we had also met on the West Africa safari. Her great sense of humour was an asset, and she took over the job of finding us hotels and restaurants for the trip south.

Our first task was to go shopping for big fat cushions, without which Isabelle would not have been able to see out of the cockpit front window, which is quite important when one is pilot in command. I have a theory that there were two principal designers of the high wing Cessna 182. One was a very tall man who designed the cockpit for his height, seeing over the top of the instrument panel and getting a clear view out of the windshield. The other designer was a man of much shorter stature, who never realised that tall people would bang their heads when walking under his wings, which were set just too low for comfort.

Our first two days flying went well, with fine weather to Maceió, which, on the way up, had been closed by bad weather. The next day we flew a long leg of three and a half hours, almost all in sunshine to Ilhéus. I say 'almost all' because the weather gods had set a trap for us at Salvador, where there were low clouds and a bunch of rain storms to keep us focused on our flying. After receiving clearance to cross the extended centrelines of Salvador's main runways, 28 and 35, we encountered cloud down to sea level with no obvious way around. One option was to divert or turn around and go back to Maceió. Second option was to fly out to sea and find a way around the edge of this rainstorm.

Finally, as there was no electrical activity in the storms, we opted to use our training to fly blind – that is on instruments only – through the cloud until we emerged on the far side. Strictly speaking, we were not legally authorised to exercise these skills in Brazilian airspace, but if you won't tell anyone, then we will keep quiet about it and hopefully we'll stay in the clear, in every sense of the word. In the end, it was only five minutes of flying inside a cloud before we emerged back into bright sunshine and clear skies for the rest of our flight to Ilhéus.

I have had some hairy, scary taxi rides in my time, but Brazilian taxi drivers take fast and reckless driving to a whole new level. High speed and sharp braking skills are essential even if there is only fifty yards to go before reaching the back of the traffic queue once more. All taxis travel at approximately nine inches from the car in front, are specialists at slalom-style weaving, and can execute a ninety degree turn, with no warning, when a possible shortcut idea bursts into the driver's consciousness. One occasionally experiences a shortcut, at high speed naturally, through the forecourt of a petrol station or some such, to gain five or even six places in the queue of traffic. I established some clear survival rules for Brazilian taxis. Firstly, never sit in the front seat next to the driver, and secondly, always wear a seatbelt. Deep breaths help, as does chanting a survival mantra – oh, and definitely hold on to something secure.

Staying overnight in Ilhéus gave us the advantage of revisiting Dos Hibiscus, the delightful small hotel set among the flame trees with their bright orange blooms, located on the edge of the beach, with its palm tree outlook. The owner, Luca, was originally from Ljubljana, and this knowledge is essential, as it was the password to access his WiFi. The bar and kitchen is run by two rather sullen local ladies who make you wait for your caipirinhas, but they cook great food, just as their mother's taught

them. Their Moqueca de Peixe e Camarão, Brazilian fish stew, is to die for.

The next day's flight to Vitória was uneventful until we landed. The airfield operators decided there was no room for us to park our tiny aircraft on this huge airfield and, after much reasoning, appealing to better natures, and looking disappointed and cross in equal measures, we finally had to take off again and went to Guarapari Aeroclub.

This is where we met Marcos. He was an instructor at the aeroclub, spoke good English, and was very helpful to us. We invited Marcos to join us for dinner that evening in this seaside town that, like all seaside towns, went into partial hibernation once their season was over. He took us to his favourite pizza restaurant and we had a great time together. Marcos was a newly qualified flying instructor, aiming to become a commercial airline pilot. He worked for half the week as a lowly paid instructor in Guarapari, and the other half of the week earned good money, to fund his flying, in Sao Paolo with his other skill as an electronics engineer.

Marcos was a jovial and chubby man and as black as the ace of spades – am I still able to say that in this age of political correctness zealots? But he was, and his forefathers probably arrived in Brazil from Mozambique or Angola as a result of the shameful Portuguese slave trade. Brazil differs from Argentina and Uruguay in the mix of ethnic backgrounds of its people. It truly is a rainbow nation and my observation was that it seems more truly integrated than any other country I have visited. Brazilians seem, in my experience, to be genuinely colour blind, and it was wonderful to see and share.

The next morning, back at the airfield, Marcos continued with his helpfulness as we discovered that there were no parking spaces available for us in the whole of Rio de Janeiro – and there are a lot of airfields in the city. We lost this argument too. No parking means no authorisation to fly into Rio until the next day, when they would squeeze us into the vast international airport, Galeão, which is the Brazilian equivalent of Heathrow or Charles de Gaulle. We decided to fly a bit further south to Cabo Frio, where its cold waters and waves are much favoured by surfers. Great fish restaurants too, and Isabelle and I enjoyed an excellent lunch where we ordered what we thought was a small dish of anchovy and prawns only to have a large grilled fish arrive at the table that would have fed a family of four for Sunday lunch. I remember enjoying it and feeling rather full all afternoon.

Authorisation to fly to Rio arrived the following morning, but the visibility was less than ideal for the flight. Air traffic control in Rio is complex, with many commercial flights arriving and departing from numerous airfields, military air traffic conducting exercises, and a myriad of heliports serving those who prefer to avoid the road congestion in their choppers. As we approached the Rio airspace, in poor visibility, we received instructions to fly to reporting points whose Portuguese names failed to register in our brains and which we could not recognise or find on the aviation charts. "Unfamiliar with the area, request vectors to the field," is a very useful phrase in such circumstances and makes life much easier. After a sequence of radio instructions such as "Fly heading 230 for six nautical miles," we heard, "Are you visual with the field in your

ten o'clock?" and we looked out to the left and, sure
enough, there was this huge airfield with runways long

enough for us to land, take off again, and still land again before the end.

I never did see that girl from Ipanema, despite maintaining a good lookout during my first and second visits to Rio. I knew that she was tall and tan and lovely and that when she walked she's like a samba and swings so cool and sways so gentle, but she was nowhere to be seen. Perhaps she was on holiday. We did revisit Corcavado, this time taking the red train, and rode the cable cars to the top of Sugar Loaf for a second time. In addition, we saw the Uruguayan street market, and gazed at the remarkable architecture, both exterior and interior, of the cathedral built in the style of a Mayan Temple. Our coffee stop was at Confeitaria Colombo, which was built in 1894, with a high ceiling of domed stained glass, large mirrored walls, ornate and dark stained wood with lighting of clustered white-bonnet glass lampshades hanging from the ceiling. The white-shirted waiters in blue checked aprons served our coffee in china cups, together with the delicious Pastel do Belém pastries. It was a visit to a bygone and elegant era.

The evening meal was at the Porcão Churrascuria in Ipanema, using our metal tongs to hold one end of the wafer of beef, cooked 'mai passada' rare, as the razor-sharp knife wielded by the waiter gently cut the meat from the cluster of steaks impaled on his sword skewer. Cut and come again is the order of the meal, and we did again and again, with a 'well maybe just one more tiny taster' indulgence. We loved it.

Having failed to land at Florianópolis on the journey north, we aimed to get there on our way back. Just one problem. Between us and Florianópolis there lay a large weather front that appeared to be going nowhere any time soon. As there was no avgas at Galeão, catering only for Jet-A1 aircraft, we needed to refuel. Our plan was to fly to Itanhaém, the pronunciation of which you would never guess from looking at the word. Suffice to say that it involves wrinkling up your nose and slipping in an 'ing' noise in the middle, followed by a 'y' immediately after it, and without sounding as if you are speaking Chinese. After lots of pre-flight practice we never got there in the end, as the cloud forced us to divert to São José, chosen partly because we could pronounce it.

I have stayed in more boring places than São José, where the main tourist attraction is the shopping mall, but I have not stayed for three days in such a place before. That was our fate, as we were weathered in. Sylvain, who is a physiotherapist in Normandy, spotted a leaflet in the hotel lobby for Milena Cabeleireiro e Estética, which offered manicures, pedicures, and massage. Thinking a massage would be relaxing and help to pass the time, he asked the reception desk if he could make an appointment. "Will it be an all night massage, sir?" asked the receptionist, much to Sylvain's surprise. That idea was dropped from the plan of things to do today.

Our hotel had two large stained glass windows either side of a portrait of the city's founding father, which summed up the place for me. On the left was a scene from 1900, when there were only green fields, farm animals grazing peacefully, crops growing, and small farm dwellings nestling in the gently rolling hills. The right hand view depicted the year 2000, where there was a scene of bustling industrialisation, crammed full of factories, roads buzzing with traffic, and with aircraft flying overhead. All the grass was gone, the animals dead, and vegetables were trucked in from elsewhere. Somehow, I wished we had been lucky enough to be here in 1900.

At long last, having used up all of our reserve days from our schedule, the clouds parted and let us see blue sky in the gaps, so we could fly above the clouds at 6,500 feet to Florianópolis.

This was a pretty location, with the main city on an island reached by a bridge from the mainland. Monika lived here so, once again, our lives were organised for us and we met another mayor and saw another exhibition and heard more speeches and saw the ground upon which the Aéropostale pilots walked. I think I was suffering from over-exposure at this point in the trip and may have been a bit tired – although not grumpy of course – after six weeks 'on the road'. Actually, 'in the air'.

The instructors at the Aeroclub de Santa Catarina, Kleber and Samuel, were great company and gave us souvenir caps with embroidered gold wings, showed us their immaculate training aircraft, and joined for the evening meal of two different dishes of cod and potatoes. Sounds weird, I know, but both were delicious, if lacking variety. Good red wine though!

The weather continued to play games with us on our departure for Pelotas. We watched a storm advancing on the airfield as we completed our pre-flight checks the following morning. We just got away in time, took a less than direct route to skirt around the edge of the incoming weather, and flew the coastline into the clear skies over Pelotas.

We met up again with Mario, a local pilot from Santos who was down to visit his mother in hospital. Mario had been very helpful during our earlier visit to Pelotas, assisting in resolving the myriad of regulatory procedures required at this entry point into Brazil. We had a great evening meal with Mario after being unable to get into our first choice restaurant because they were offering a special 'Ladies Night' deal, and the queue spread outside the churrascaria and down the street with not a man in sight. Perhaps we had a lucky escape?

Wednesday 28 May, we filled out the myriad of forms needed to leave Brazil and enter Uruguay. We flew over the Rio Jaguarão that forms part of the boundary between the two countries and we were in Uruguayan airspace once more, with formalities with customs, immigration,

and police to look forward to at Angel S. Adami airport once again.

We had our farewell dinner that night, in Montevideo, for on the following day we would be making our separate ways home.

It had been an unforgettable adventure.

Over my seven weeks in South America, I had flown just a smidgen shy of 80 hours. Assuming an average air speed of 110 knots, say 125 mph, then I had flown close to 10,000 statute miles. That is almost enough to fly from London to Brisbane.

Some journey. Some adventure.

"So if I lived my life alone, without anyone that I could really talk to, until I had an accident with my plane in the Desert of Sahara, six years ago. Something was broken in my engine. And as I had with me neither mechanic nor any passengers, I set myself to attempt the difficult repairs all alone. It was a question of life and death for me: I had scarcely enough drinking water to last a week....... Thus you can imagine my amazement, at sunrise, when I was awakened by an odd little voice.........I saw a most extraordinary small person, who stood there examining me with great seriousness. Here you may see my best portrait that, later, I was able to make of him. But my drawing is certainly very much less charming than its model." so writes Saint Exupéry in his book *The Little Prince.*

My last story, in this book, again is an adventure shared with the Raid Latécoère charity that supports French schools amongst the former colonies of France. Madagascar was a French colony which in 1960 was given the opportunity, together with its much smaller Indian Ocean island sister, Réunion, to make the democratic choice to become part of France or gain their independence.

Madagascar chose independence and Réunion decided to become a region of France, albeit a bit detached from the French mainland. The contrast between these two islands today is dramatic. Réunion is modern and wealthy and looks like any other Region of France, such as Provence or Aquitaine, whilst retaining its own individuality. Madagascar on the other hand is a poor country, a very poor country with the French infrastructures of roads, rail, airports, and utilities having been left to decay. The promises of the wealth and prosperity from independence seem today to have been a deception. Such a beautiful island yet so sad.

I have found no evidence that Saint Exupéry ever travelled to the then French colony of Madagascar, although it is not inconceivable, for within his book, The Little Prince, he incorporates the Giant Baobab which is the landmark national tree of Madagascar.

To quote from his book, "*Now there were some terrible seeds on the planet that was the home of the little prince; and these were the seeds of the baobab. The soil of the planet is infested with them. A baobab is something you will never, never be able to get rid of if you attend to it too late. It spreads over the entire planet. It bores clear through it with its roots. And if the planet is too small, and the baobabs are too many, they split it into pieces.*"

In 2015, I teamed up with Robin and Isabelle again. This fourth and final story of the book, "Baptême de

l'Air", is set in Madagascar with the added ingredient of sharing the delight and spontaneity for life that young children gift to us.

Baptême de l'Air
Madagascar June 2015

It was a fine day, with a chance of a few isolated showers as we sat in our aircraft at the Tolagnaro airfield of Fort Dauphin, making final checks before taking off to fly north along the eastern coastline of Madagascar. We had two flights scheduled for the day. The first leg was 184 nautical miles to Manakara for refuelling, then a further 252 miles to Tamatave.

As forecast, we started to meet the odd shower cloud after a hundred miles, and these were easily skirted around, although they were getting a little less isolated by now. In fact, we began to suspect that there might be a shower cloud convention gathering ahead, as our horizon became more and more misty. The next cloud we encountered seemed larger than normal, and, flying out to sea, we were unable to find a way around it. We cut back inland to seek a passage on the left hand side but were equally blocked so, following a radio chat between the two aircraft, it was decided to land at a diversionary airfield and wait for the weather to clear.

Farafangana was the nearest airfield and Robin and I were the first aircraft to arrive, but we could not land as the local children used the runway as their cycle track and were racing up and down as we did our low pass, causing the cyclists to scatter for cover. Completing our circuit and returning for a second landing run, we had a clear runway with an audience, and their bikes, watching from the sidelines.

The airfield was deserted, not counting the playful children, so with both aircraft on the ground now we found dusty old chairs to sit on and wait for clearer skies.

Robin went for a walk and encountered a local lady, carrying a sack, walking across the airfield. Eager to try his emergent Malagasy language skills, Robin stopped to chat with the lady and asked, mostly in sign language, what she had in her sack, upon which the lady thrust her hand inside the sack and produced a live duck secured at the legs with string. And so the negotiation began. How much was Robin prepared to pay to buy the duck? Somehow, Robin found a way to extract himself from this situation without buying the duck. I really must keep a closer eye on him, especially as I had promised his wife, Lety, I'd make sure he did not get into trouble!

Robin Wicks and I had flown together in South America last year, so our 2015 adventure was to join the French pilots on another Raid Latécoère flying trip, this one around the old French colony of Madagascar. Sitting in the Indian Ocean just off the coast of Mozambique in Southeast Africa, it is easy to misjudge the size of Madagascar. It is almost as big as France and only a tad short of three times the size of Great Britain. Twenty-two million people live in the Republic of Madagascar, so we had plenty to keep us occupied on this two week flying trip.

This year, the other trips organised by Raid Latécoère proved more popular, so we were only two aircraft. The second crew were my friend Isabelle Grimaud, from Réunion Island, Bernard Morieul, who I had met on the trip to Senegal, and a newly qualified French pilot, Benjamin Vignal, whose job was to be responsible for flying planning and logistics.

As ever on these overseas trips, our first tasks were to obtain the pilot's licence for the country and do a flight test in the hired aircraft to the satisfaction of the examining instructor, as well as a myriad of other bits and pieces of aviation authority administration. This year's extra treat was to attend a lecture on the meteorology of Madagascar which, as it was all in French, meant I lost all the finer points as well as some of the blunt ones too. I did get the bit that said the island had big mountains in the middle and the rain fell mainly on the east coast! We were then given an exam paper, in French, the questions of which were on topics not covered by the lecture and addressed weather issues encountered by airline pilots flying above 30,000 feet! Not something a private pilot in a single-engined propeller aircraft comes across much. Somehow, we all passed!

We were hiring our aircraft from the airfield for the capital city of Madagascar, Antananarivo known as 'Tana', as it's too much of a mouthful for most visitors to master the pronunciation. Our flight tests were deferred while our aircraft, a Cessna 182 Mike Delta Foxtrot, completed its maintenance. The other crew were fortunate in that their Piper Comanche, Mike Echo Lima, was serviceable, and they could get going on the task of meeting the examiners' exacting flying standards. Finally, our aircraft was flyable – you notice I avoid the accolade of 'serviceable', since this implies that everything works, which it didn't, save for the essentials like an engine, a propeller, two wings, and one radio.

The owner was an airline pilot with Air Madagascar (or Air Mad as it styles itself – may need a new marketing person there!), Enrico Boto. Enrico was a busy man and had three mobile phones, one of which was always active, so he became adept at holding conversations with you whilst talking on one of his phones and telling a second phone to "Hold on". We guessed one phone was for business and one for personal calls but the third one was a mystery until our French friends explained, and they would know, that the third was for his mistress!

And so it was that during my flight test with Enrico he spent the whole time on the ground, and in the air, talking on his mobiles, and my flying instructions were conveyed with casual hand movements. I took off, flew round for a bit, avoided flying over the president's house (absolutely top priority), and landed without a word spoken to me – and I had passed!

Friday 19 June, three days after leaving England, we were ready to fly. Our first flight was a short one of 72 miles due south to Antsirabe, also set in the mountains at 5,000 feet above sea level. This was to be the first stop at which we would take school children on their first flights or, as the French say more poetically, their 'baptême de l'air'. We were met at the airport by teachers, parents, and twelve school children who looked both excited and a little nervous. It was their big day. Madagascar is a very poor country – very poor – so to have the chance to fly in an aeroplane is way beyond their wildest dreams. Even to go to school is a privilege. All education has to be paid for, with the exception of the wonderful SOS Children's Villages charity, which provides education for children whose families are too poor to pay for their education. In the large towns, maybe thirty percent of children are educated. In the countryside, it will be way lower than that.

These twelve children had been chosen by their teachers on the basis of their outstanding work and achievements. We took two children at a time, each pair sitting on the back seat of the aircraft being flown by two pilots. The baptême de l'air flight consists of a take-off, climb to 1000 feet, flying a rectangular pattern, and landing back six minutes later, then taxiing to the waiting parents.

To put the children at their ease, Robin and I collected each pair, held their hands as we walked to the plane, and strapped them into their seats. Language was limited as only a very few speak French and we speak virtually no Malagasy. So it was smiles, touching fists, thumbs up, and hand waving to put them at their ease. It worked with most, who relaxed and enjoyed the experience, but a few retained an anxiety. But what a tale they have to tell their friends when the flight is done. Each aircraft does three flights and on our third flight, I noticed a school below where all the children had left their classrooms and were in the playgrounds, hundreds of eyes watching us. Must beat learning about Pythagoras or osmosis!

Later, we were taken to the SOS Children's Village and School, where all the pupils, three to four hundred of them in their blue smocks, were seated on the ground and rose to welcome us. A group of a dozen girls, and one boy, performed a delightful and funky dance in our honour. A beautiful day.

The following day there was low cloud, barely 1,500 feet above our heads as we drove to Antsirabe airfield. We had a flight across the mountains to the western town of Morondava, but with clouds hiding our view of those mountains it was unwise to take off. After an hour or so we could see some lighter spots, and with the forecast that the cloud did not stretch far to the west, we could see a way through by following a river valley. We climbed to 8,500 feet and sat above the cloud in bright blue sky and, more importantly, above the highest mountain peaks, giving us a clear flight.

Roads in Madagascar are unlike any in Europe. Tarmac roads, where they exist, have not been maintained since the country voted for independence from France in 1960. As a consequence, the function of the tarmac nowadays is to hold the potholes together. Traffic is hard to describe unless seen at first hand, but imagine roads filled with handcarts, rickshaws, cycle rickshaws, tuc tucs, white vans in use as buses, lorries, bullock carts, cars, zebu cattle, goats, dogs, bicycles, motorbikes, women carrying their loads on their heads and children, children, children, all teeming and merging gently as they progress to their destinations.

Unlike the boys, who were just there for the flying and the Three Horses beer, Isabelle had read up about places to visit in Madagascar and told us that we just had to visit the Allée des Baobabs. I knew that baobabs were called the upside-down tree, as it looks as if their leafy tops are beneath the ground, with their roots waving at the sky, but that was the sum of my knowledge of these trees. So we took taxis for the long bumpy drive to the tree avenue.

A bony bum is not one's best features for road travel in Madagascar, I reflected, as we left the potholed tarmac road after forty minutes of bumpy ride for the uneven and equally potholed dirt track. Ylang ylang orchards lined the road, their trees having been deliberately stunted by breaking the leading boughs to create uneven umbrella shapes, so that the yellow flowers could be harvested without the use of a ladder, to make the romantically scented perfume.

An hour later, we arrived to find the baobabs, the national tree of Madagascar, which, as previously mentioned, appear in Saint Exupéry's book, *The Little Prince*. The trees are silent giants of the forest, towering

high above the other trees and reaching ninety to one hundred feet in height. Although we had passed occasional baobabs on our drive, it was impressive to find an avenue of these friendly monsters. We walked among the trees, photographing them from many angles before stopping by a rickety stall to buy a polished wood carving of two baobabs that had grown entwined around each other, the 'lover baobabs'. The stall was run by a family whose shack was made of stick and mud walls, a dried grass roof, and with the casserole cooking over an open fire outside.

A beautiful young Madagascan woman, in her late twenties and surrounded by children, was seated on the earth having her hair braided by her mother. She already had eight children and this was well below the average family size of ten to twelve children in Madagascar. This would explain why we see so many children, and I was told that children make up nearly seventy percent of the 22 million people in Madagascar. Clearly there is a huge market for television sets in Madagascar, once there is electricity widely available, and that might slow down the birth rate here!

Bernard had a penchant for asking, with a cheeky smile, the sort of personal question reserved for late night risqué television interviews. He set off to ask one woman if she was pregnant, which elicited a strong word of caution from Robin. "Not a question a man should ever ask a woman," advised Robin. "I made the mistake once and never again." Bernard went ahead and asked the question anyway! Thank goodness I had not promised Bernard's wife that I would keep him out of trouble. Mission impossible.

We watched the sunset from across a small lake, covered in water lilies, with the giant baobabs standing out like dark sentinels in the colourful twilight, with its pink and orange sky.

From Morondava, we flew south to Tulear or 'Toliary', in the Malagasy language. The coastline is an endless ribbon of tropical paradise beaches, mostly deserted. We saw large forests of green with thousands of baobab trees dotted throughout, standing like giants amongst their diminutive relatives.

We had twelve school children waiting for us and their 'Baptism' flights. They were brought to us, holding hands with our guide Faneva for their flights. Afterwards, we gathered in the tiny airport terminal to hear a delightful speech of thanks from their teacher and we were each presented with a colourful conical-shaped straw hat, by the children, as a personal thank you for their day in the air.

We enjoyed a lunch of delicious grilled capitan fish accompanied by THB beer, which always tastes so refreshing after a few hours flying. We explored the small African town in the afternoon. Nobody clears rubbish from the streets so plastic bottles, paper, cloth, and general waste is left to lie around. The streets are simply dirt roads with small makeshift shacks alongside to sell second-hand clothes, local handmade furniture, vegetables, or meat that is laid out on wooden slats, attracting the attention of inquisitive flies. Only cakes and bread are kept under plastic covers. The centre of the street was filled with traders selling their produce or goods from a cloth laid directly on the ground.

It is relatively easy to set up a 'shop'. You just sit on a spare piece of dirt street and start repairing a bike. Soon, people appear with their rusted and ancient bikes that need repair and your new business is up and running. No rates, no rent, no buildings to maintain, no electricity or running water, and at the end of the day you pack away your spanner and tin of oil and ride your bike home. The bicycle shop is now closed until tomorrow morning.

Robin decided to take a constitutional walk around the town later that afternoon. Walking past one building, he could hear gospel singers and went inside to satisfy his curiosity. It turned out to be a church service being held in a shed and the choir was in full voice. Robin took a chair to enjoy the singing. At the end of the song, the pastor, having spotted a new convert enter the church service, decided it was time for a rousing sermon directed mainly at Robin. Now trapped within the worshippers, Robin was unsure how to extricate himself from this dilemma. The sermon showed no signs of ending quickly, so Robin crouched low and crept to the front of the service, put money onto the offertory plate, and shuffled backwards out into the street. Once again, he had slipped from under my watchful radar!

To get to Fort Dauphin, also known as Tôlanaro or Tolagnaro, in the south east corner of Madagascar, you can simply fly anticlockwise around the coastline, as did Mike Echo Lima, or take the direct route shortcut across the foothills of the mountains, which saves sixty miles. Robin and I had a slower aircraft than the Comanche, so we decided on the shortcut and both aircraft arrived at

Fort Dauphin more or less together. Twelve more excited children were there for their first flights with us.

Zebu cattle, which hail from South Asia and are characterised by a fatty hump on their shoulders, as well as floppy ears and a dewlap, seemed to be the principal breed of cattle on the island. Indeed, that's all we saw. Unfortunately for the Zebu, it has the juiciest and tastiest of meat. So during our stay on Madagascar it is fair to say that a substantial quantity of Zebu steak and chips were consumed between us. Goes really well with a full-bodied red wine, too!

The following day was the one of the rain showers, the diversion to Farafangana grass airfield, and Robin's duck-buying incident. We did get away from Farafangana, after waiting three and a half hours, and set off to fly the remaining one hundred miles to Tamatave, where twelve more excited children had been waiting patiently for their flights.

But first, we had to make a refuelling stop at Manakara. This proved to be an extended stop, as with no refuelling facilities available we had to siphon aviation fuel from the steel drums into plastic containers and then pour them into our fuel tanks by hand. This took a long time, and with daylight becoming limited, we elected to stay the night in Manakara.

The best hotel in town, all two and a half stars of it, was the Hotel Sidi. At least it was a bed for the night, although the ornate deep red satin bedspreads were more reminiscent of a bygone era or, so I've heard tell, a house of ill repute. We enjoyed looking around the local market, the paths between the crowded stalls being just wide enough for one person, leaving very restricted passing room. As darkness descended, the stall owners continued to trade by candlelight or, on the posher stalls, the occasional low wattage bulb run off batteries.

Wednesday 24 June, we made an early start to fly to Tamatave but once more met an impenetrable wall of rain cloud, forcing a second diversion to Mahanoro. Its grass runway finally came into view at 500 feet under the cloud. Once again, we were the big event of the day, with over twenty village children quickly arriving to stare at us. The children gathered around 'Uncle Robin', who, speaking in English, played a 'Say After Me' game with them. The children spoke no other language than Malagasy, yet, like

153

all children, they had well-attuned ears and enjoyed repeating the unfamiliar sounds in a singsong unison.

After a while, Robin decided to end this game, and said "That's the end," and walked away. "That's the end," chorused the children, and emulated his walking away steps. Which gave Robin a new idea. He taught them, on the command of "Aaah-tenshun," to come smartly to attention, salute, and shout "Sir!" After a few goes, they were drilled to perfection, laughing and giggling with delight. If Robin ever needs a new career, there is clearly one in children's entertainment.

Whilst this was happening, the French were most anxious, because it was lunch time and there was no food. Luckily, a few villagers had joined the children and, using Faneva's language skills, one villager, who had a moped, was despatched to the village to buy bonbons for the children, as well as chicken and rice to make lunch for ourselves. While waiting for the moped man to return, the villagers set about lighting a bonfire and boiling water, in readiness for the rice, and making a barbecue, using scrap bits of metal lying around, for the chicken.

At last the moped man reappeared and, to our surprise, the chicken was still alive! Bernard came into his own here and, getting out his trusty camping knife, he set about preparing the chicken, cutting it up, and grilling it on the barbecue. The rice preparation was delegated to the villagers. And so we had a rather late lunch of very scrawny and tough roasted chicken, accompanied by pink rice. By the time the makeshift lunch was eaten, the weather had cleared sufficiently for us to finally complete our journey to Tamatave.

The next day, we were grounded in Tamatave by overcast low cloud and rain showers thwarting our plans to fly to Diego Suarez at the top of the island. Bored pilots – and pilots do get bored when all they can do is spend the day looking upwards hoping for the weather to improve enough for flying. After lunch, Isabelle and I decided to take a cycle rickshaw ride, for an hour or so, around the town after negotiating a 10,000 Ariary fare. It might sound a lot of money, and it probably was the rip-off tourist rate, but as it only equated to £2, we were happy and the rickshaw man was very happy too.

The 10,000 Ariary note is the largest denomination bill in Madagascan currency. You can buy a lot of food and goods with that. Often, it is too big for traders to change (or so they say!). In any case, you don't really want the change, as it is so worn and dirty that it looks like a health hazard. When applying for my pilot's licence with the Civil Aviation Authority in Tana, the fee required was one million Ariary, and they would only accept cash!!! This necessitated quite a few visits to a cash machine, and there are not many of those around, especially working ones.

The next morning saw an improvement in the weather, but a cloud bank persisted across the north east coast, barring our way to Diego Suarez. So we decided to change our plans and fly due west over the mountains to Majunga on the sunny west coast. Most towns in Madagascar have two names, which can be quite confusing. One is the French name and the second is the local Malagasy word. So Majunga is also known as Mahajanga.

Majunga airfield is not very large at all and we were the only two aircraft there, but the security staff did not allow that to get in the way of their over ambitious rules and procedures. Hence, we were met on landing by security and the baggage crew, who insisted on loading our bags on to a trolley and walking with us across the tarmac to the terminal, where the security guard directed us through the passenger door, while our bags went through an adjacent baggage door. Inside the terminal, we watched the baggage staff, no more than ten yards away, take our bags off their trolley and load them onto a moving baggage belt, to make the short journey back to us.

It was a national holiday to celebrate Independence Day in Madagascar. Crowds of people were streaming to the city centre to enjoy the amusements and celebrations. At seven in the evening, it being dark at that time in the Tropics, the firework display began, which we all watched from our hotel as a continual flow of families with excited

children, squeezed into diminutive tuc tucs, filled the road. The tuc tucs merged in with young couples on scooters, occasional cars, white van buses, and hundreds of people in their party dress walking with the children, who waved streamers.

After dinner, Robin, Benjamin, and Bernard decided to take their own tuc tuc ride into the centre of town, and so it was that I let Robin out of my sight again as I relaxed and sipped my glass of Cognac digestif with Isabelle in the 'comfy' lounge chairs.

The centre of town was heaving with happy people buying food from the stalls, children going on the simple fairground rides, and adults drinking and chattering while competing with the pop music blasting out over the loudspeakers. The tuc tuc could only crawl at a snail's pace, at best, through the crowds. Robin, wanting to savour the infectious atmosphere more closely, suggested they walk around for a bit, but Bernard and Benjamin were somewhat unsure of the wisdom of this.

So Robin let them return to the hotel, whilst he would make his way back later. Now Robin did stand out in this crowd, being much taller than the average Madagascans, a lot whiter, and wearing distinctive European dress. However, everyone was having fun and Robin was joining in with a smile here and some French greeting there, whilst searching for an ice cream vendor – when all of a sudden there was a power cut, the music stopped, and the square was thrust into that inky blackness that makes the stars shine so brightly. Corporal Jones' immortal words

'Don't Panic' came to mind as people allowed their eyes to adjust to what little light may be coming from the moon. Luckily, after ten minutes or so, power was restored and all was well again.

Next morning, we had the pleasure of meeting more smiling children who were excited about making their first flights with us. Robin and I always kept a sick bag in our pockets in case these were needed in a hurry, but the occasion for their swift deployment, fortunately, did not arrive. After our three flights around the circuit were complete, and photos and thanks likewise completed, we set off north for the small holiday island of Nosy Be. We were told that Nosy Be meant 'Big Island' in Malagasy, which makes one wonder what they call Madagascar. Probably 'the absolutely humongously ginormous unbelievably vast island that is bigger than anything around with the possible exception of Greenland, New Guinea, and Borneo and they are miles away anyway'!

The following day was a rest day on Nosy Be, so what to do? This proved to be no problem, as Isabelle had found there was a Nature Reserve with lemurs in the wild. I was up for this, although the other boys seemed more attracted by hiring motor scooters and driving around the island for the day.

Olivio was our guide to the Lokobe reserve, and he arrived at the hotel promptly at eight thirty, just as we were finishing our breakfast. I liked Olivio, who had a positive view of life, reflected in his answering questions with "Not yet".

"Have you been to England, Olivio?"

"Not yet."

"Have you been to France, Olivio?"

"Not yet."

"Are you married, Olivio?"

"Not yet."

I just loved this attitude to life. Anything he had not done was just another thing he was waiting to happen to him one day in the future.

The Lokobe Nature Reserve was at the tip of the bay but only accessible by boat, so first we needed to take a taxi to Ambatozavavy on the shoreline, where our boat awaited us. Almost an hour later, having been driven, in our taxi, through Hell – the curiously named capital of

Nosy Be – we arrived at Ambatozavavy, where all we could see were outrigger canoes floating near the shore. Removing our shoes and socks we waded out to the pirogue, as the wooden canoe is known, and climbed on board. Olivio was in the front, Isabelle behind him, then me, with our taxi driver at the rear. We all had paddles and when not paddling my job was to bale the water from inside the boat so we could complete the forty-five minute journey across the bay without sinking, before reaching the tiny settlement of Ampasiphony at the edge of the forest.

The villagers had produced a sumptuous lunch for its two guests, way too much for us to eat. This problem was easily solved when all the food we had left was used to feed the rest of the village, with quite a bit left over for tomorrow!

Time to search for lemurs. Olivio explained that we would be in the forest for about an hour and a half and that it was essential to maintain absolute silence so as not to frighten off the wild animals. The forest had dense vegetation and Olivio carried his 'meso be', or big knife, to use as a machete if the undergrowth became impenetrable. Before long, our guide had spotted a lemur high in the branches of the trees. This one was a reddish brown colour and not the usual ring-tailed species one sees in photos or Disney's *Madagascar* film. The brown lemurs were females, we were told, with the males being black. Lemurs are tree dwelling, like monkeys, and have cat-like features.

Later, perched in the fork of a tree's branches, sat an example of another species of lemurs, smaller, furry, Christmas-pudding-shaped with large eyes, blinking in the forest light, as this one was nocturnal and had been rudely awoken by our guide.

There are no deadly animals in the Madagascar forests, although a boa constrictor could give you a nasty squeeze. We spotted a couple of them. One was asleep, curled around a tree trunk, about half way up, and the second was on the ground with a very large bulge in its stomach. Probably just swallowed a lemur, and it would not be moving for some days until this meal was digested.

Olivio, and the taxi driver, were most adept at spotting wildlife, so would point out chameleons and pick up tiny frogs, geckos, and lizards with bright yellow, green, or iridescent purple colourations. Birds flew about our heads, weaving in and out of the trees with effortless and consummate flying skills. The meso be knife was used to slash one large green succulent plant from which spewed a bucketful of fresh water. Not surprisingly, this potential life saver was known as the traveller's tree, or ravenala madagascariensis. The popular name sounded a bit more catchy to me.

We got back, two hours later, to relate our day's tales and hear of the others' exploits on their scooter tour of Nosy Be.

On Monday, 29 June, we flew to Diego Suarez, also called Antsiranana, on the northern tip of the island, where again we stayed for two days. By now, Isabelle was our established tour organiser, and our first trip was to the Tsingy Rouges rock formations.

We set off on the two hour drive after lunch at the Hotel de la Poste. The drive was two hours, due more to the poor state of the roads than the distance. The driver's way of dealing with the uneven and potholed roads was to use whatever part of the on-road or off-road surfaces afforded the least bumping of his passengers. This method has to also take account of the opposite direction traffic, using similar pothole avoidance techniques, providing frequent opportunity for head-on collisions. At times like these, a last minute decision by both parties to belatedly assume the right hand rule of the road avoids collision, but one does need to be skilled in millimetre-sized near misses for success.

The last seventeen kilometres of the journey were on a sand road that descended steeply to the floor of the huge valley with occasional severe inclines. You have probably seen programmes on television where four wheel drive vehicles accept the challenge of an impossible mountainside track strewn with boulders and craters for which not all succeed. Well, it was rather like that, except we, in our beat-up old taxi, were now competitors within the challenge and not mere spectators.

It was with a sense of relief that we finally arrived at the valley floor, although we did realise that we were going to have to brave the return journey if we were not to be sleeping outdoors tonight. Surprisingly, there was a man at the bottom, in a makeshift hut, who collected our tickets. He clearly has an arduous journey to work that puts our grumbling about the weekday traffic jams driving to London into a clear perspective.

The spectacle before us was worth the nail-biting journey. The scene was a sea of red sandstone-like rock that resembled bunch after huge bunch of asparagus. Geologists term the rock as laterite, it being rich in iron oxides and aluminium, and the strange shapes are the result of tropical weathering. The visual effect is truly mesmerising and we wandered around them, taking photographs.

The following day, we set off to visit the Mer d'Emeraude by boat. Martine met us at the hotel at seven in the morning and led us through the back streets, down a narrow alleyway, to the muddy water's edge, where our faint hope that our boat might be a luxury yacht was quickly dispelled. Shoes off again, trousers rolled up above the knee, we waded slowly and unsteadily over the slippery pebble-strewn seabed to our simple fishing boat, whose fitting out consisted only of wooden planks across the beam of the boat, where we could perch, holding our position by locking our feet on the ribs of the wooden hull.

The outboard motor was fired up and we set off across the Baie Andovobazaha to the Indian Ocean and the Emerald Sea. The captain set course for the northern shore of the bay, where we picked up the cook and her provisions, waiting on the beach. Back at sea, and with the wind picking up, we raised the sail, watching as it arched artistically in the breeze and took us to the mouth of the bay, which led out into the Indian Ocean. Here we waited, for a large rock and sand bar guarded the entrance to the bay and this could only be crossed at high tide. We waited and watched fishermen wading in the shallow waters over the rocks, looking for seafood catches.

Judging the tide was sufficiently in, our skipper carefully steered across the barely submerged rocks with his crewman hanging over the bow of the boat, giving hand signals left or right. Back in deep waters, the sail was hoisted again, and we tracked towards a distant island. About a third of the way across, the sea colour made a dramatic and instantaneous change from a dark, oily, and opaque green colour to the brightest and clearest emerald, a colour you would

only see otherwise in the gemstone glinting in sunlight.
A beautiful sight.

Martine cooked a scrumptious barbecue fish, crab, and chicken lunch, with fried sweet potato and rice, on our desert island, where we relaxed, walked, and snoozed for two hours before heading back.

On the first of July, a Wednesday, we headed back to return our aircraft in Antananarivo. We couldn't resist a small detour after departure to take one last look at the Emerald Sea, this time from the air, before flying to Majunga for refuelling. It was just after one o'clock when we landed back on Tana, after twenty-five hours flying around this beautiful island, with time to relax.

We were greeted by our final group of twelve schoolchildren, awaiting their flights. Three more take-offs, three more landings, and six more happy children's faces. They'd experienced, for perhaps the only time in their lives, what it was like to fly up with the birds. Perhaps, just perhaps, we might have inspired one or two to work hard and achieve their own dreams by becoming pilots too.

Derek Alway

Final Thoughts

The Little Prince book first appeared in 1943, its story based on Saint Exupéry's crash in the Sahara desert. Later in 1943, Saint Exupéry rejoined his Free French air squadron in northern Africa. Despite being forbidden to fly (he was still suffering physically from his earlier plane crashes), Saint Exupéry insisted on being given a mission. On July 31, 1944, he set out on a reconnaissance mission in his twin-engined Lockheed Lightning from Borgo Airfield on the island of Corsica, to overfly occupied France.

He never returned.

In 1998, a fisherman found his identity bracelet in the sea south of Marseille.

Parts of the aircraft were recovered in 2003.

Lightning Source UK Ltd.
Milton Keynes UK
UKHW020222020223
416313UK00002B/34